25

D1034663

Fulfill thy Ministry

Fulfill thy Ministry

by

Stephen C. Neill

Harper & Brothers, Publishers
New York

FULFILL THY MINISTRY

Library of Congress catalog card number: 51-11944

Contents

Preface

THE chapters which follow were first given as lectures at a conference of the Inter-Seminary Movement held at Rock Island, Illinois, in January, 1950. Wire recordings of four of the lectures were taken at the time, and I have kindly been supplied with a transcript from these recordings. The lectures were delivered from short notes, and in a deliberately conversational style; as I expected, they have had to be entirely rewritten, since what is effective in speech can be intolerable on the printed page. But I have tried not to depart too far from the original style, and, as the reader will quickly discover, this book bears no resemblance to a theological treatise.

To my surprise, the wire recordings of my lectures have been played over many times to audiences of theological students in a number of seminaries. This leads me to hope that some of the things which I have written may be found relevant to the needs of American theological students, and may be of use to those who are preparing themselves for the most glorious career in the world.

S. C. N.

Geneva, Switzerland
June, 1951

7

Fulfill thy Ministry

⚔ 1 ⚔

The Minister and His God

I

THE simple chapters which follow are not written sermons; but, as an aid to memory, I have planned to take a verse of Scripture as our starting point for each one. We begin with the ninth verse of the fourth chapter of the Second Book of Kings.

Since my boyhood, I have been a student of good literature in a number of languages. I would affirm with some confidence that, from the point of view of narrative brilliance and effectiveness, there are few things in the literature of the world that can equal and none that can excel the stories of the Old Testament. In the Old Testament nothing surpasses the narratives of the Books of Kings. In the Books of Kings, nothing surpasses this story of the woman of Shunem and her little son—concise, monosyllabic, vivid, moving in its very simplicity. However, today we are not concerned with the brilliance of literary technique, nor with the touching story of the boy who went out to join the reapers and cried out, "My head, my head," and lay on his mother's knees till noon, and then died. We are concerned only with this sketch of the character of Elisha, clear and economical as a good etching. "I perceive that this is a holy man of God, that passeth by us continually."

Elisha had received, so we are told, a double portion of the spirit of his master Elijah; but he had not inherited the explosive and volcanic character of his predecessor. He was a pastoral prophet, going on his rounds from place to place, and caring for the people; and just for that reason he is a more instructive model for us, who are much more likely to be called to just such a quiet pastoral ministry than to wrestle with the prophets of Baal on the top of Mount Carmel. As he passed by from time to time, this wealthy lady of Shunem saw him, took note of him, and summed up his character in this way: "I perceive that this is a holy man of God, that passeth by us continually."

How did she know? Surely the answer is that, when you meet a holy man of God, you do just know, by an immediate intuition that is very difficult to break down into simpler terms or intellectual categories.

When I was in India, almost all the Indian ministers who worked with me had at least ten or a dozen villages under their care; that meant that like Elisha, they had to go on their rounds, sometimes on foot, sometimes on a bullock cart—maximum speed two and a half miles an hour, the nearest thing to eternity that I have ever experienced in this world of time—sometimes, in these up-to-date days, on a bicycle. Although Christians were fairly numerous in our part, they had to pass through many villages in which there were no Christians, and which were entirely inhabited by Hindus or Moslems. I used to say to those brethren, "Unless the non-Christians say of you, 'We perceive that this is a holy man of God, that passeth by us continually,' you are not doing your job." I would say the same to you. If, by God's grace, you come in time to be ordained and to have a church or parish of your own, you will be surrounded by many people who are not churchgoers. Unless they say of you—not your own people, but the outsiders—"This is a holy man of God," you will not be doing your job, either.

This brief phrase sums up our whole subject. That is what it means to be a minister—to be a holy man of God. This is a humbling and terrifying thought.

II

I doubt not that, in your own experience, you can think of a small number of men and women to whom that phrase really applied. As we look back over the history of the Church, we meet a few men and women who were made great by the greatness of their experience of God.

A sympathetic English historian, Bernard Manning, who was a Congregationalist, has written in those terms of Luther; Luther was great just by reason of the greatness of his experience of God. Luther was not great, as was John Calvin, in the realm of dogmatic theology. You can indeed work out a system of Lutheran dogmatics; but in order to do so, you have to read rather a large proportion of the eighty volumes of the Weimar edition of his works. He was not great as an organizer. If he had been more gifted in that direction, the Lutheran churches would have stood up better against the waves and storms of the Counter Reformation. No, what above all else we find in Luther is a permanently memorable experience of the grace of God. It is all there written in the record of his life; the yearning and striving after acquaintance with a gracious God; the agony of not finding him; and then the great revelation, which beats and pulsates in Luther's great hymns, and even in page after page of his most theological writings, that the righteousness of God is not that justice by which he punishes sinners, but that tender mercy, through which he seeks and finds sinners, and saves them through faith in Jesus Christ the Crucified.

Look much further back in history and you will find the same phenomenon in the prophets of Israel—men made great by the greatness of their experience of God.

It is interesting to note that the majority of the prophets were what today we should call laymen. Among them all, only Jeremiah and Ezekiel were priests. Amos was a shepherd on the hills of Judaea. Hosea and Micah appear to have been countryfolk and small farmers. Isaiah, whose name suggests that he was of kin to the royal family, was a town dweller and a statesman. If we, as theological students, are called to be holy, certainly we have no monopoly of that vocation. Yet surely I am right in stressing this as peculiarly a part of our calling, since the very aim and purpose of our ministry is that all the people of God may be led in the way of holiness.

Note again that the prophets' experience of God was not a remote and mystical business, involving separation from the concerns and interests of ordinary men. It was precisely the opposite. They lived where men lived. In their pages, you can hear the echo of all the ordinary concerns of men—the noise of the market place, the thud and tread of armies marching and countermarching in their campaigns. It was their intense concern about social righteousness and the destinies of nations that drove them back upon God in searching and questioning, and finally to the revelation of the truth.

The little book of Amos can be read slowly and carefully in twenty minutes. If you read it attentively, I think you will find in it the record of his discovery of God, or, as we should put it more theologically and correctly, of God's revelation of himself to him.

High on those Judaean uplands, Amos must often have watched his flocks by night, like those other shepherds, centuries later, of whom we also read in Scripture. His book shows that, as he did so, he watched the stars wheeling overhead and sinking beneath the waters of the Great Sea, brighter and clearer than in our foggy northern atmospheres. Sometimes, when it is exceptionally clear in Europe or America, I say to myself, "This is almost like India," and I feel homesick for those more brilliant constellations of tropic climes. As Amos watched them, they spoke to him of the Creator of heaven and earth, who holds those wheeling systems in the hollow of his hand. "Seek him that maketh the Pleiades and Orion, and turneth the shadow of death into the morning, and maketh the day dark with night; that calleth for the waters of the sea, and poureth them out upon the face of the earth; the Lord is his name."

Round the campfire at night, no doubt they talked, as shepherds will, and told old tales of the great acts of God in ancient times. I suppose that, in the days of Amos, very little had been written down of those ancient traditions of the race, and of that little, hardly anything can have been in circulation in shepherd camps. It was the long memory of the East that kept those stories alive in the minds of men. And so they recalled how in ancient times the land had been inhabited by the Amorite "whose height was like the height of the cedars, and he was strong as the oaks"; and how God brought a rabble of slaves out of Egypt and led them forty years through the wilderness, and then set them on the incredibly hazardous enterprise of crossing the Jordan and taking in possession the land of a people of a higher civilization than their own; and yet it had been the Amorite, who for all his strength had gone down in defeat because the Lord "destroyed his fruit from above, and his roots from beneath." Israel always lived in the memory of those great events. There was always among them the sense of

a God who is active in history, of a God who directly
takes a hand in the affairs of men.

From that Judaean escarpment, you can look away to
the western sea, over one of the great trade routes of the
world. That little flat strip of the Shephelah, leading on
to the cities that are now called Haifa and Beirut, and to
ancient Antioch, is still immensely important in the
affairs of men. I suppose that sometimes on clear days
Amos could see the sunlight gilding the tips of spears
and lances as the soldiers went by; Egypt against Assyria,
Assyria against Egypt; with all the intervening kingdoms
waiting in anxious suspense, joining sometimes one side
and sometimes the other, ineluctably drawn into the
perennial drama of this history of the nations. Men had
often seen that before. But Amos looked upon it with
new eyes. He was the God of Israel; but was he the God
of Israel only? "Are ye not as the children of the Ethio-
pians unto me, O children of Israel? saith the Lord. Have
not I brought up Israel out of the land of Egypt, and the
Philistines from Caphtor and the Syrians from Kir?" All
these tumultuous nations are his concern. The interna-
tional scene is also a sphere in which he is perpetually at
work.

Sometimes Amos would go down from his uplands to
the cities, to Jerusalem and Samaria, and would be horrified by what he saw of the wickedness of men. His
burning phrases ring as though new-minted today. There
were the rich, who oppressed the poor with false weights

and high rates of interest and oppressive mortgages, who would sell a man and his family into slavery, "for a pair of shoes," because they could not pay a trivial debt; those who lived easily and luxuriously, "but are not grieved for the affliction of Joseph."

Gradually these four aspects of the experience of God —the power of God in nature, the redeeming activity of God in history, the providence of God in the affairs of nations, the judgment of God on all the ungodliness and righteousness of men—are fused together at white heat in the mind of Amos. They make a driving power that will not let him stay. Although he is not a prophet nor a prophet's son, with no professional qualifications or training, the Lord drives him out, saying "Prophesy unto my people Israel."

III

If you in your day and generation are to be a prophet of the Lord, I do not think that you will need more than these four experiences that came to your predecessor of twenty-six centuries ago; though of course those experiences will come to you with far richer content, because of the manifestation of the glory of God in the face of Jesus Christ, and of the accumulated riches of the experience of the Church through nineteen centuries.

Look out, with the eyes of imagination and faith, on this good world that God has made, and see him in it. It *is* true that "the heavens declare the glory of God." But see him not only in the tender colors of the spring and the glowing colors of the sunset. See him active also in the wonderful work of the scientist, as slowly and patiently he brings to light mysteries that God had hidden from the time of the creation of the world. Unhappily, the attitude of many scientists has made us think of science almost as an enemy to religion. That ought not so to be. Every scientist worthy of the name, whether he knows it or not, is really our colleague in the service of God. Nuclear fission and atomic energy are words that strike terror to our hearts; but chiefly because, when this amazing new power was put into the hands of men, the first use they chose to make of it was so abominably wicked. Surely, our first thought should be of wonder, at the apparently illimitable energy that God has locked up from the beginning of time in our universe, and our second of admiration at the wonderful patience and ingenuity of men, slowly tracking down the mystery, finding the key, and at last setting the energy free for the use of men. And our thought may well turn itself into a prayer that, for once, mankind may exercise just a little common sense, and learn to harness this new power to the service of men and not to their destruction.

Secondly, learn to look back on history as the record of the great acts of God. Whatever we may make of the Christian faith—and in loyalty to the different confessions to which we belong, we shall be bound to make of it slightly different things—none of us has any right to treat it as anything but a historical religion. This is what distinguishes it from religions such as Hinduism or

Buddhism, which are primarily systems of ideas. Our faith goes back to certain things which we are assured God did—those very ancient things that he did in bringing Israel out of Egypt and making a rabble of slaves into a nation; those less ancient things he did, when a man was born and was known as Jesus of Nazareth, and wrought certain works and spoke certain words, and suffered certain things, all in a determinable epoch of human history. There is always a temptation to simplify the Christian faith into an idea or a philosophy or a system of doctrine or a tradition. If you are to be faithful, you must never do any of these things; you must never detach the faith from its historical character. The God whom we are called to proclaim is the *living* God, the God who acts, who is still actively at work through the Holy Spirit, who does not repeat the things that were done once for all, but goes on doing the same kind of things, and is prepared to do them, here and now, in this very year, in the very place where you have been called to serve.

Thirdly, as you climb, like Amos, to your high place, and look out on the strange tormented scene of the nations of the world, be assured that, through the smoke and noise and confusion, God is working his purpose out, not only in the narrow stream of the life of the Church, which will be our primary responsibility, but also on the great scale in the larger issues of world history. We live in a time of breaking and remaking. Nations, races, classes long suppressed are making their voices heard, successfully claiming a place in the sun, vindicating their right to take a full share in the common life of the nations. What God is doing in our time we can only dimly discern. We can see in part that his Word that is going forth in our time is of judgment on an unfaithful Church, of warning to a materialistic civilization, and of promise for a better and more righteous ordering of the affairs of men.

Then turn your eyes back from the distant scene to the world at your feet. Wherever you are placed, you will not have to look beyond the boundaries of your own city or community or village to find some form of social injustice or oppression. This seems to be part of our human condition, and, I am afraid, will be until the end of the world; when evil in one form is cast out, it strangely reconstitutes itself in another. In your area, it may be harsh treatment of young criminals, or lack of proper care for the insane, or bad race relations, or unnecessary tension between capital and labor. All such things must be among the primary concerns of the Church. Too often we are blind to them; but as Christians, we have no right to be blind, and to say that we did not know. In whatever garden of Eden it may be your good fortune to be placed, there will certainly be a serpent. If you are a minister of the Gospel, you have business with that serpent.

Here, then, is the prophet's fourfold experience of God, as Creator, as Redeemer, as Ruler, and as Judge. In the next chapter we shall consider the more subjective side of this experience, as it works itself out inwardly in self-surrender and vocation. Here we are thinking of the divine activity that takes hold on men and sends them out to proclaim the Word of the Lord. Amos on his Judaean height meets God and he goes forth to say to Israel and Judah, "Thus saith the Lord."

IV

How did he know that it was the Word of the Lord, and how did the people know that it was the Word of the Lord?

Alas, there can be no mathematical certainty. There are true prophets and false prophets. You will find in the Old Testament, and especially in the Book of Jeremiah, many records of the conflicts between them. It is always possible that the prophet may be self-deceived; it is always possible that the people may follow a will-o'-the-wisp and be lost. It is only the aftertime that can pass judgment on the prophet's work. There is always an element of adventure, of peril, in every human attempt to declare the Word of God.

We know that Amos was not self-deceived because, century after century, his words have continued to echo in the hearts of men and to affirm themselves as the truth, because they correspond to and illumine the realities of the world and of the life of men as men must live it, because they are true to the highest that men can receive of the nature of the living God, because they have in them dynamic power to educate the conscience and to strengthen the will of the hearers. These are the real marks of inspiration.

It is far easier for us than it was for Amos. We have an objective standard in the records of Scripture, in the words and works of Jesus Christ himself, in the conscience of the Church through the centuries. And therefore, recognizing in all humility the possibility that we may be self-deceived, we yet dare to affirm that it is the will of God that when we stand in the pulpit, we should be clothed with like authority, that we should be able to say "Thus saith the Lord," and that the hearts and wills of men should affirm that we have spoken the truth of God.

There is an immense difference between speaking with authority and speaking from authorities. Some preachers have an irritating habit of backing up every statement that they make with a quotation: "as Kierkegaard has said," or whoever may be the fancy of the day. This puts them in the same category as the Jewish scribes. It was their habit to say, "This is the word of Rabbi X., who heard it from Rabbi Y., who heard it from Rabbi Z.," and so on every occasion to produce their catena of witnesses. For this reason, when Jesus said simply, "I say unto you," the people heard him with astonishment, because he spoke as one having authority, and not as the scribes.

It is true that we are also "scribes who have been made disciples unto the kingdom of heaven." We have at our disposal all the treasures of Christian theology. If you are ordained, you will enter the pulpit not as an individual, but as the accredited representative of a church. But it is well not to obtrude the secondary authorities. The Word of God will not come to life on your lips, unless it is a word that you have encountered and experienced and lived, unless you are able to say, "Thus saith the Lord." If you are able to speak in this way, men's hearts will bear you witness that you speak the truth, and, whether they will hear or whether they will forbear, they will know that there has been a prophet among them.

At this point, some of my readers may be inclined to say that I am pitching the work of the ministry far too high. After all, Amos and Isaiah, Augustine and Luther and all the rest of them, were religious geniuses. To suppose that we could do the same work would hardly be the expression of religious humility. In one sense this is true. It is unlikely that any one of us will make a decisive mark on history. But it seems to me that the objection needs to be rather closely considered.

Has there ever been such a thing as a religious genius? I am not sure.

Certainly, there have been men of genius who have been men of faith. If the man of genius dedicates all his powers to the service of Christ, it may well be that he will break out in such memorable utterance as will echo all down the centuries of time.

Augustine of Hippo was certainly a literary genius. As a young man, before his conversion, he had received the best training in literature and rhetoric that his time afforded. Thus, one of the treasures that he was able to bring to the service of Christ was a magnificent gift of eloquence; and when, after his conversion, his whole being was aflame with the love of God, he was able to pen those memorable pages of the *Confessions* that to this day stand among the most moving of Christian documents.

Johann Sebastian Bach was, I suppose, the greatest musician who has ever lived. He must have been, also, a man of intense and childlike faith. If you have any music in you at all, to listen to one of his great compositions is a religious experience of almost unbearable poignancy. Not long ago I heard again his *Passion According to St. John*, rendered in one of the ugliest concert halls in the world before a thoroughly secular audience. Yet such was the power of the music that, if at the end the conductor had turned round and said, "Let us pray," I do not think that any one would have been surprised.

John Bunyan, the simple tinker of Bedford, was endowed with the mysterious gifts of directness of vision and perfect simplicity of style. The *Pilgrim's Progress* is perhaps, next to the Bible, the favorite book of the Christian world.

I am sure, however, that in the case of these men and others like them, the genius and the religion were separate things, brought together by a conscious act of the will, by the deliberate dedication of all their gifts to the service of Christ.

It may also be true, and probably is, that there are some men who have a special gift for religious experience —who find it easy to believe and to be good. This is also a gift from God, but I am not convinced that it is a specially valuable one. Look at history and consider the men and women who have rendered most conspicuous service to Christ and his Church. Do we not find in most cases that they were men whose hearts were naturally as hard as the nether millstone, who had had to wrestle with every conceivable kind of doubt, who had early become entangled in evil habit or base desire, and had found no easy way of deliverance? It sometimes seems as though God for his own glory had chosen the most unsuitable instruments and, out of their unsuitability, out of the intensity of their conflicts, out of their very weaknesses and defeats, had fashioned the strength that was to make their work memorable in the history of the Church.

V

Apply this to yourself. God does need variety of gifts and equipment for the fulfillment of his work. If you have special gifts of intellectual power, or artistic sensitiveness, or administrative ability, all those are things that can and should be consecrated to the service of God. But do not for a moment imagine that the possession of such gifts will of itself make you an effective minister. If you are one of those who are naturally religious, who find it easy to pray and to feel the presence of God, be thankful that you are delivered from the agonies that some others have to pass through; but again, do not imagine that such gifts will of themselves make you effective in the service of Christ. If, on the other hand, you know that you have no special gift of brain or hand or tongue, if you do not find it easy to be good, if you fight and are defeated and fight again, if you sometimes wonder whether it is worth while to go on at all, do not for a moment be downhearted; none of these things means that you lack what is essential for the service of the ministry. The one essential thing is spiritual power. And that, I believe, is available to every one of us, if only we are willing to pay the price.

During the course of these addresses, I shall have a good deal to say of the principle, *sola gratia,* by grace only. That which we could never have of ourselves, God of his infinite goodness supplies. On that truth rest all our hopes. And yet there is another side. It is quite evident in this world that God will do nothing for us that we can do for ourselves. There are many things which we may have, but only if we are willing to pay for them. God is a just salesman; there are no bargain counters in his store. You can have almost anything that you want; but you will not get anything at all, unless you are prepared to pay the fair price for it.

The knowledge of God, which makes men prophets, the spiritual power which makes them effective ministers, are, under one aspect, gifts of God's grace alone; yet under another, they are good merchandise for which a fair price has to be paid. That is what puts them within the reach of us all, if only we are willing to pay the price.

If you look back to earlier days in the history of the Church, I think you will find an earnestness in this matter that is far from common among us today. Look, for example, at the early records of the Student Christian Movement. Then it was assumed that the all-important thing was that a man should seek God with all his heart, wrestle with God, know God, be filled with God. It was taken for granted that, if you were a Christian at all, you would have a quiet time of an hour for private prayer and Bible study every morning, quite apart from what you might do in the way of going to services in church or Christian Union meetings and the rest. My mother has told me that, in four years as a medical student at Edinburgh, she never once missed her hour of quiet before breakfast—and in Edinburgh in winter the temperature can go down to 0° Fahrenheit, and there is no central heating. If you talk to people of the age of my parents about those early days, they will recall how John R. Mott was going round the world, telling people that they must have *unhurried* time to wait upon God. "Unhurried" is the word that comes back to them as specially characteristic of the time.

In 1945 Dr. Mott, looking back over fifty years of the World Student Christian Federation, wrote for *The Student World* an enthralling article entitled *Recollections of Pioneering Days*. Part of it is concerned with the famous student conference at Mount Hermon in

1886, from which so much of contemporary Christian work among students has sprung. Dr. Mott writes:

> Unlike some of our present-day meetings, when people can hardly give up a complete week-end, our conference lasted for twenty-eight days, and all the students stayed the whole time. We had only one meeting a day and D. L. Moody always presided. . . . The rest of the day was spent in small groups, or delegation meetings, or simply in thinking out what we had heard and out under the elm trees plying the leaders with vital questions. And as the spirit of the conference deepened, we spent our time in thought and prayer into the watches of the night.

I miss something of that spirit of earnest seeking in most of our modern conferences. There are so many meetings, such pressure to get documents written and resolutions passed, such weariness of body and spirit, that sometimes human activity seems to have been made a substitute for the working of the Spirit of God. I sometimes wonder how, in the Christian world of today, anyone ever finds time to say his prayers; sometimes I have an uncomfortable feeling that I know the answer.

Some time ago one of my brother bishops in England went to have a Turkish bath. While he was wearing about as much as one does wear in a Turkish bath, the attendant, who was doing to him whatever attendants do in a Turkish bath, said, "Excuse me, sir, but I think you are a clergyman." The bishop was a little surprised, not knowing what there was particularly recognizable about him at that moment; the attendant explained: "Ah, sir, it's always the knees that give you away." I could wish that that were true of all of us. One of the bitterest things I have ever heard in my life was a remark made concerning another bishop, who in his day was a great leader in the ecumenical movement, "The man isn't at home on his knees."

Theoretically, we all admit the primary claim that God has on our time; but there is usually a chasm between theory and practice. And there is a tendency for theological students to say, "It will be all right after ordination; then it will be my substantive job, and it will be far easier to find time for it than it is now." Let me assure you that that is not so; it is what you do now that is all-important. After you are ordained, throughout your ministry till your retirement, and even after that, you will find that the temptation that never leaves you is that of allowing anything else in the world to take the place of the primary obligation to seek God and to hear his voice, and that your constantly renewed and bitterest struggle will be so to order your time that God really has the first place in your life. It is so easy to justify ourselves. There are many things to do; there are the claims of the Church and its organizations, of family and friends; so many useful, trivial things to do. Unless you have formed disciplined habits of prayer as a student, and unless from the beginning of your ministry you set your face like a flint against everything that can disorganize those habits, you will find that within three years, your time of waiting upon God has been whittled away to practically nothing. And then good-by to your chance of speaking the Word of God with prophetic power.

VI

There are many parts of prayer. Later on I shall discuss intercession. But now we are concerned only with the habit of being still in the presence of God and looking at him. You may remember that lovely verse of the Psalms: "They looked unto him and were lightened"; or *were radiant*, as another translation gives it. That is our part. To look unto him, stilled, patient, aware, until he is pleased to show himself to us. We must be prepared for those many occasions on which God is silent, and does not specially reveal himself to us; we must not be impatient, or suppose that God can be commanded by our importunity. But if we wait, we have reason to expect that God who commanded the light to shine out of darkness will shine in our hearts to give the knowledge of his glory in the face of Jesus Christ.

I am told that the present generation does not read the poetry of Robert Browning. If so, so much the worse for the present generation. But it may be that you are not familiar with the poem, *Rudel to the Lady of Tripoli.*

Rudel was a troubador, who had fallen helplessly in love with the Lady of Tripoli (that is, the Tripoli in Syria, one of the Crusader strongholds) who, he knew, could never be his. Finding a pilgrim setting out for the East, he bids him take a message to the lady concerning a mountain and a flower. At the foot of the mountain is a foolish flower that, as the sun passes overhead, always turns its face to him:

> and in the lost endeavour
> To live his life, has parted one by one,
> With all a flower's true graces, for the grace
> Of being but a foolish mimic sun,
> With ray-like florets round a disk-like face.
> Men nobly call by many a name the Mount
> As over many a land of theirs its large
> Calm front of snow, like a triumphal targe
> Is reared, and still with old names fresh names vie,
> Each to its proper praise and own account:
> Men call the Flower the Sunflower, sportively.
> . . . .
> Dear Pilgrim, art thou for the East indeed?
> Go!—saying ever as thou dost proceed,
> That I, French Rudel, choose for my device
> A Sunflower outspread like a sacrifice
> Before its idol.

You will grasp at once the meaning of Rudel's emblem. You will grasp equally the application of it that I have made to our waiting upon God. I have chosen an illustration from secular literature; I might equally well have chosen one from Scripture: "We all, with unveiled face reflecting as in a mirror the glory of the Lord, are transformed into the same image from glory to glory, even as from the Lord the Spirit." If you ever decide to preach on that text, as I hope you will, you will find that every single word in it needs to be carefully studied and pondered. But the general idea is clear. Memory comes

back to me from schooldays of a certain house on a hill
four miles away that at a certain moment toward sunset
would catch in its windows the level rays of the sun, and
throw them back over the plain in a glory of living gold.
Scripture tells us that Christ came into the world to
bring grace for grace, that the word of God is proclaimed from faith to faith, and that it is his will that we
should be transformed from glory to glory.

This transformation, after all, is nothing less than to
be transfigured into recognizable likeness to Jesus Christ;
and to be transfigured after his likeness is to become a
holy man of God.

VII

As we were traveling to Rock Island, some one said
rather unkindly, "You can easily tell who are going to
the conference; you can pick out a Seminary student half
a mile away."

I am afraid that that unkind person was not thinking
of the inner radiance and outward glow of which we
have been speaking. But it would be surprising if, at your
present age, you were able to manifest it, since it is a
thing that only comes with time. What you should have
now is the brightness and freshness of early experience
of Christ. But that is something that will pass away.
There are hardness and frustration and disappointment in
the work of the ministry. These things will leave their
marks on your faces and write lines about your eyes. But
in place of that first freshness there can and should come,

and will come, if you are patient and desire it and are willing to pay the price, that inner radiance, that stamp of unmistakable likeness to Christ, that holiness which comes from dwelling in God through him.

Do not think of this holiness as negative, as merely the abstention from certain kinds of sin. I have some friends who I think might be saved if only they could commit one large sin; then they would at least have committed themselves to something. Christian holiness is not negative but positive. It means taking hold of Christ in continually renewed self-dedication to his will. It results in such quiet mastery over life, without timidity and without aggression, as is seen in Christ himself in the pages of the Gospels.

This is the one thing which you will never be able to counterfeit. By the time that you have been three years in the ministry, you will be able to counterfeit almost everything else. You will be able, with very little preparation, to get up into the pulpit and preach a sermon that will make all the kind ladies in the congregation say, as they pass you at the door, "Doctor, that was wonderful." You will be able, especially if you have a devoted secretary, to put on the appearance of the busy administrator, always so concerned with the affairs of his parish as to have no time to rest, though in reality you may be effecting very little. Without being very much of a hypocrite, you can act and play a part and keep up appearances. The inner radiance of intimate fellowship with God is a thing that you can never counterfeit; and those who themselves know God will know infallibly whether you have it or not.

Each of you will form his own ideal of the ministry, and it is good that it should be so, since there are diversities of gifts and diversities of needs in the Church. But whatever ideal you may form, this must be the central pillar in it—holiness, without which no man can see the Lord, likeness to Christ, without which no man can be the messenger of Christ. If you have this, does anything else matter very much? You may never be more than a second-rate preacher. You may have no special administrative gift. Your absent-mindedness may drive your elders to distraction. But if I should chance to visit your parish and on asking, "What kind of a minister have you here?", should receive the answer, "We perceive that this is a holy man of God that passeth by us continually," should I worry much about anything else? Wherever likeness to Christ is seen, even dimly, in minister and people, we know that God's name is being glorified, his purpose is going forward, and his will is beginning to be done on earth as it is in heaven.

❧ 2 ❧

The Minister and Himself

I

"But thou desirest truth in the inward parts." (Psalm 51.)

This seems to me one of the most searching words in the whole of Scripture. Truth—honesty in the inward parts. If a man will be honest with himself, there is practically nothing that you cannot do with him; if he will not be honest with himself, not even God can do anything for him. "If we walk in the light, as he is in the light"—these words clarify what I am trying to say. God is all of a piece with himself and so must we be. To walk in the light is to be transparent to God, and to ourselves, and to other people, without evasion and without concealment. Without that transparency there can be no true Christian life; there certainly can be no effective ministry.

Shortly before I left England I was talking to a very fine candidate for the ministry, and he said to me, "What is it that happens to ministers at about the age of forty?" He had gone, with a number of fellow students, on a preaching mission in one of our great industrial cities, and had noticed, in his work in various parishes, that after forty a great many ministers seem to lose initiative and enthusiasm and enterprise. As he looked forward to his own ministry, remembering that probably all those men whose work he had been watching had started on their course with such enthusiasm as his own, he wondered whether the same thing would inevitably happen to him, or whether there was some means by which that fate could be avoided.

About the same time, I was traveling by train with two fellow bishops, one of whom is exactly my age, the other a little younger. We agreed that the years between forty and fifty are the most dangerous in a man's life. Everyone recognizes that in those years a woman is passing through one of the great crises of her life; it is not so generally recognized that just the same is true of a man. After forty, physical reactions are slower than before, and in most men capacity to stand up to severe physical strain is markedly less. The mind grows less supple and resilient. Few men have any new ideas after the age of forty. (Some men, of course, have no new ideas after they leave the seminary. Why should they, they know it all!) If you study the lives of the great thinkers, you will find that almost all of them—A. N. Whitehead is a conspicuous exception—had arrived at their chief discoveries before the age of forty, though they may have spent many years after that developing them in detail and working out their applications.

It is not that there is anything specially critical in those years in themselves. It is just that, as every psychologist knows, that is the time at which inner weaknesses are most likely to show themselves. In most normally healthy people, the physical vigor of youth and of the adventurous years will carry them through to about the age of forty. Then, as the power of resistance grows less, any inner weaknesses that there are will certainly show themselves, with consequences that may be physically, mentally and spiritually very serious. If that is so, and since the ministry is bound to be a career of special strains and temptations, it is far better to find out now while we are young whatever inner weaknesses there may be, and to let them be dealt with by the grace of God and by common sense, rather than to let the years wear us down, and bring out the weaknesses, just at the time when we ought to be growing into leaders and pillars in the Church. "Thou desirest truth in the inward parts."

II

The first point at which we have to exercise this scrupulous honesty is the question of vocation. Why do you wish to be ordained? Let us immediately put on one side all the conventional or fancy reasons, which you might express to a church board or a presbytery, if that question were put to you. You know as well as I, and probably the wiser among your teachers have emphasized this point, that, if we are quite honest with ourselves, we may find some less satisfactory motives under-

False motives

lying the more satisfactory and plausible ones on which we prefer to dwell.

One wrong motive which may enter in is the tame acceptance of a tradition. Some young men are brought up to the idea that they will enter the ministry. When the time comes, they tend to acquiesce in the idea rather than to make a deliberate and personal choice. This danger is perhaps greater in the families of ministers than elsewhere, but is certainly not limited to them.

I had a friend who went through four years of training for the ministry. I could never detect in him any sign of a real vocation. And then, at last and in time, he discovered it himself. Not long ago he told me how it had come about. When he was twelve or thirteen he announced, as boys will, that he was going to enter the ministry. His parents, pious lay folk, leaped on the idea with delight and from that moment on, he was steadily trained and groomed for eventual ordination. Having finished his military service, he entered the seminary and spent four years of increasing unhappiness, the reason for which he steadily concealed from himself. Then one day he woke up to reality, and discovered that ordination was not in the least what he really wanted. He had the good sense and the courage to cut loose and take up a secular career, in which he is doing very well, and experienced an immediate sense of deliverance. I shall not be at all surprised, however, if after some years of that work he discovers that there is something in him which cannot be satisfied except by the work of the ministry. But it would have been disastrous if he had gone straight into the ministry without this time of spiritual leisure in which to distinguish the false motives from the true.

We used to have a great deal of trouble in India over this business of vocation externally induced. If in an Indian Christian family, several girls were born before a boy (you will understand what this means, when I mention that in my Indian language the proverbial expression for a situation of great gloom is, "Like a house in which a girl baby has been born"), or if a couple had long remained childless and then received the gift of a boy, it would almost invariably happen that the boy would be dedicated to the service of the Lord, and of course christened Samuel. Twenty years later a wholly unsuitable young man would turn up and inform us that he had been dedicated to the Lord from birth, and therefore must be taken for the work of the ministry. The present bishop of Madras used to say that, if ever I became a bishop, I would excommunicate any parent who christened a child Samuel! The idea is admirable, but there are right and wrong ways of carrying it out. I am myself the son of a minister; I know that all of us were dedicated to God's service by my parents before we were born. But we were never told so until we were grown up, with the result that our family has produced two ministers and three missionaries.

If, when you are honest with yourself, you recognize that family tradition, the wishes of parents, perhaps a certain amount of moral pressure, have played their part in your being here as a candidate for the ministry, do not immediately conclude that your vocation is a sham. The tradition of godliness in a family is a glorious inheritance. I look back with thankfulness on five generations of austere Presbyterian piety in the family of my Scottish mother. (I don't think that the Irish part of me has contributed much to the promotion of godliness.) If you have such a heritage, rejoice in it. But remember that in the crisis of decision, all such extraneous things have to be put aside. True vocation to the ministry is a matter of personal, independent decision in the sight of God. By that personal decision you must stand or fall.

In some alleged vocations to the ministry there is, perhaps unrecognized, a desire to escape from the hardness of life. An outstanding French psychologist has told me that in France since the war there have been few vocations to the parochial ministry of the Roman Catholic Church, and a good many to the monastic life; but that, in his judgment, many of these monastic vocations were neurotic and escapist rather than genuine.

You and I know, at least I trust that you know already, that the life of the ordained minister cannot escape gigantic perils and temptations of which the layman knows nothing. But it is also true that, from the point of view of the ordinary man, the life of the minister is a sheltered life. He is saved from some of the roughnesses and hardnesses of life. He is exempt from the risks which are the daily bread of the businessman. He is not faced by the ethical dilemmas by which the Christian layman is confronted in our tormented industrial civilization. It is possible that when we are entirely honest, we may find that deep down in us there is something of this desire to escape. I remember a great leader in my own church saying a good many years ago of a candidate for the ministry, "Yes, I think X. had better be ordained; he hasn't the guts to make a good Christian layman." This was a cruel remark, yet obviously it deserves to be thought over.

2A

If you find that mixed up with your sense of vocation to the ministry, there is the desire to take the easier way, I can assure you that there is one thing and one only to be done. Finish your seminary training, and then go and earn your living for two years as a layman in a fairly tough job. There would be advantages in every candidate for the ministry being required to go through such an experience. I do not mean such expedients as earning a few dollars during student vacations. Still less do I mean semiclerical occupations, such as Y.M.C.A. secretaryships, honorable as these are in their kind. Service in the armed forces provides the opportunity of meeting with all sorts and conditions of men on an equal footing and learning their minds; but there the problem of earning a living does not arise. No, I mean just the kind of life that is led by the great majority of lay folks in and outside our churches, where hard knocks have to be taken and risks run, and not infrequently poverty to be endured. If, after a year or two of such work, you were to find that the idea of the ministry was fading from your mind, and

that the real field of your vocation was the lay world,
there would be no need to feel that you were turning
your back on God or betraying your own highest ideals;
one of the greatest needs of the Church is more laymen
who will really live out the Christian life in the place
where ordinary men live and do their work. But if,
having proved yourself in such a sphere, you still feel
that the work of the ministry is your work, you can
return to it with far greater confidence that your sense
of vocation is a gift from God, and not wishful thinking
or self-deception.

The third insidious motive that may from the start
corrupt the purity of vocation is ambition. After all, to
be up in the pulpit is a fine thing; it makes a man the
center of attention and puts him in control of the situation. That is what many men obscurely desire—to have
the eyes of others upon them, to be in control of the
situation. In fact, in the pulpit you are more in control
of the situation than anywhere else; unless your sermons
are exceptionally bad, the congregation will not answer
back, and you are safe from the worse things than back
answers that might befall you on the political platform,
or in the rough world of industry and labor. Now if, in
the honest self-scrutiny that we are all trying to achieve
here, God shows you that there is a core of ambition in
your sense of vocation, resolve that you will not venture
to be ordained, until God has shown you that this central
sin in motive has wholly been taken away.

Ambition means the concentration of thought and

attention on self. As long as that self is present and alive, not crucified with Christ, you may be everything that is admirable, but you cannot be a minister of the Gospel, since all the time you will in reality be exalting yourself and not glorifying Christ. "Cromwell, I charge thee, fling away ambition; By that sin fell the angels," says Cardinal Wolsey in Shakespeare's *Henry VIII*. By that sin, how many ministers have fallen!

The onset of it is so insidious, especially in our situation. It is so easy to confuse our own advancement with the glory of God. It only takes a very little self-deception to feel that all we are seeking is a sphere in which our special gifts can be better used for the glory of God. Sometimes a loving wife can be a corrupter with her "Dear, isn't it time you were beginning to look for a larger sphere?" But the moment we begin to be affected by this slight astigmatism, the integrity of our whole vision is destroyed. Nor is this a sin which we can conquer once for all by a single act of resolution. At any time it can return, with the same tireless persistence as the dust which somehow will settle on the minister's study table; it can be dealt with only in the same way. And woe betide the minister who once allows the dust to settle.

You must often have encountered the ambitious type of minister. Such a man is always restless and never happy. All the time he has one eye on another church, with better pay and prospects or a more congenial atmosphere; therefore, it is impossible to be single-minded and contented in the work that he is doing. He tends to speak often in church meetings and synods in order to have the eyes of others on him as a coming man. His thoughts and actions tend to be determined not by the will of God but by what others are likely to think, and particularly by the current policies of the leaders of the Church. Well, it says in Scripture that a double-minded man is unstable in all his ways and that such a man will receive nothing of the Lord. You can well see that the entering in of ambition spells disaster to the true work of the minister.

For the Christian there is one place and one only—the lowest place. That is the command of the Lord, and it is binding upon us all. As you enter on the work of the ministry you must seek the place of hardest work, greatest sacrifice and least recognition, and there you must be content. Obviously in the Church some men must come to the top; the places of great influence and responsibility must be filled. But woe to the Church if they are filled by the ambitious who have sought them. If when you are toiling contentedly in the lower place those who have authority to call men to special spheres in the Lord's vineyard come to you and say, "Friend, come up higher; this place of greater eminence and heavier responsibility is the one in which you can now best serve," you may accept the call without fear and without anxiety; but never, never, never, if you have yourself desired or sought what is called advancement in the Church.

III

If you have agreed with what I have said so far, you will have reached the conclusion that in this matter of vocation to the ministry, we must take nothing for granted. The more I come to know of theological seminaries the more I regard them as dangerous places. Once you are admitted as a student in a seminary it is so easy to take yourself for granted as a suitable candidate for the ministry. It is easy for your professors also and for your fellow students to take you for granted. Once admitted within the sacred circle, you are at once exposed to the temptation to play up to the atmosphere by which you are surrounded, to play up to other people's expectation of you, perhaps even to play up to your own idea of what you ought to be. Could there be any more direct road to losing the truth of your own inner being? "Thou desirest truth in the inward parts."

The process of absolutely honest self-examination is always painful. But, if you feel yourself called to embark upon it, do not let yourself become a prey to over-anxious fear. You might well come to me and say, "I find that in my sense of vocation there are elements of all the three false motives of which you have spoken." You might add evidence of hesitant faith, of serious failure in personal conduct, of instability of will, of an undisciplined heart. Would I then say, "Clearly that is the end; this way is not for you"? On the contrary, I should say, "Let us be prepared to begin again at the beginning.

After we have been willing to throw away several bushels of chaff, we may yet find a few handfuls of the good grain of true vocation; and we have it on good authority that for certain purposes a grain of mustard seed is sufficient." It is not failure that matters, but refusal to recognize failure. We have said already that if a man is willing to be honest, there is hardly anything that God cannot do for him. To be willing to start afresh demands humility; but humility is always the door of hope.

IV

We have spent a good deal of time setting forth what vocation is not. We must now turn to the more difficult problem of defining what it is. How do we recognize true vocation when we see it, in ourselves or in others?

There can be no single or simple answer, since we are all different from one another, and God has his own special way of dealing with each of us. To some, the call to the ministry comes as a very gradual strengthening of inner conviction, to others as response to a public appeal for service, to yet others as a sudden inner experience of unshakable obligation.

A friend of mine who now occupies a leading position in the Church of England told me years ago that he could point to the very spot in a street in Cairo where, when he was serving as a regular officer in the British Army, our Lord spoke to him and told him he was to be ordained. Like St. Paul who said, "Wherefore, O King Agrippa, I was not disobedient unto the heavenly vision," he felt that this was a call that could not be disobeyed. He resigned his commission in the Army. Although considerably beyond the usual age of students, he entered the University of Cambridge as an undergraduate, and after taking an exceptionally brilliant degree in theology (97 per cent for one paper on the philosophy of religion) was ordained to the ministry of the Church.

You will find a rather similar experience recorded in the life of Archbishop Lang of Canterbury, which has recently been published. A friend started the turmoil by saying to him, "After all, why shouldn't you be ordained?"—a hard question to put to one of the most brilliant young men of his day. Lang had just embarked on the career of a lawyer which, if he had gone forward in it, would almost certainly have brought him one day to the position of Lord Chancellor or Lord Chief Justice of England. The question, once posed, would not let him rest. One Sunday evening in 1889 he walked over from Oxford to the church at Cuddesdon:

The whole scene is indelibly impressed on my memory. I sat in the second pew from the pulpit, then on the north side. I paid little attention to the service, and less to the sermon, preached, I don't know what about, by the curate. But I had a strong sense that something was about to happen. I was not in the least excited; there was no sort of nervous tension; I had only prayed in rather a weary way during the service in some such manner as this—"I can't go on with this strange struggle. End it, O God, one way or another. If there *is* anything real, any-

thing of Thy will in this question, help me to answer it."
Then suddenly, while the unheeded sermon went on, I
was gripped by a clear conviction. It had all the strength
of a masterful inward voice. "You are wanted. You are
called. You must obey."

I knew at once that the thing was settled. . . . That
night in my rooms at All Souls I prayed as I had never
prayed in my life before. But all my prayers had the one
refrain: "I obey and I am free." Later the words came
to my mind: "I will run the way of Thy Commandments,
when thou hast set my heart at liberty." [1]

I have given that rather long quotation, partly because
it sets before you a good example of a vocation suddenly
made clear and accepted in a moment, but also because it
admirably expresses something that you will commonly
find in the experience of the men of God. When the call
of God comes, it is not by any means always welcome to
the one who is called.

Think again of those prophets of the Old Testament
on whom God laid his hand. They did not immediately
rejoice in the thought that it was a glorious thing to be a
prophet of the Lord. "Who am I that I should go unto
Pharaoh, and that I should bring forth the children of
Israel out of Egypt? Oh Lord, I am not eloquent, neither
heretofore, nor since thou hast spoken unto thy servant; for I am slow of speech and of a slow tongue."
"Ah, Lord God, behold I cannot speak; for I am a child.
But the Lord said unto me, Say not I am a child; for to

[1] J. G. Lockhart, *Cosmo Gordon Lang* (London, 1949), pp.
64–65.

whomsoever I shall send thee thou shalt go, and what-soever I shall command thee thou shalt speak."

In such hesitation, there may be found two motives which are not very creditable, and one which is wholly creditable.

The first of the less creditable motives is reluctance to turn away from the lights and the dazzlement of worldly success. In order to become the prophet of God, Moses had first to make that choice which is briefly spoken of in the Epistle to the Hebrews, when "he refused to be called the son of Pharaoh's daughter; choosing rather to be evil entreated with the people of God than to enjoy the pleasures of sin for a season; accounting the reproach of Christ greater riches than the treasures of Egypt." they tell us nowadays that the Christian front is all one front, and that in principle there is no difference between Fifth Avenue and the swamps of tropical Africa. I notice that that point of view is more often expressed by those who have remained on Fifth Avenue than by those who have endured the searing agony of forsaking every-thing to go to tropical Africa, and I sometimes wonder whether they are right. There are rewards to be won in tropical Africa that you cannot have on Fifth Avenue. I have no doubt at all that Dr. Albert Schweitzer, look-ing back on half a lifetime at Lambaréné, would tell you that it was infinitely worth while to have left his great career as theologian and as musician to serve as a mis-sionary doctor among primitive and rather degraded peoples. But I do not suppose for a moment that he found it easy. However, that is neither here nor there; whether it is Cosmo Gordon Lang or Albert Schweitzer, or Moses or Jeremiah of old, on whom God lays his hand and says, "You are wanted," it is only the coward soul that draws back.

The second less creditable motive is fear of what may happen, if one follows the call of God. Jeremiah knew quite well that being a prophet in Jerusalem in the seventh century B.C. would be an unpleasant and even dangerous business. It turned out to be, in fact, far worse than the worst he had imagined. When he stood up to his knees in the accumulated mire at the bottom of the dungeon in the court of the guard, wondering how long it would be before he sank right into it over head and neck, he may well have wondered whether he would not have done better to say No to God's calling at the start. I do not suppose that any minister who takes a strong line in the social obligations of the Gospel is likely to be permanently popular. God gives us no guarantee at all that we will not suffer. Yet I can see no reason why those who feel called to the ministry should allow their fears to determine their conduct, and should bargain for an easier passage than those who are called to the service of their country in time of war.

The creditable motive is fear before the very greatness of the task to which we are called. It is, after all, a terrifying thing to be called to take a special responsibility for the souls of men. Any man who is ordained to the ministry of the Episcopal Church hears at the very time of his ordination the following words:

And now again we exhort you, in the Name of our Lord Jesus Christ, that you have in remembrance into how high a dignity, and to how weighty an office and charge ye are called; that is to say, to be messengers, watchmen and stewards of the Lord; to teach and to premonish, to feed and provide for the Lord's family; to seek for Christ's sheep that are dispersed abroad, and for his children who are in the midst of this naughty world, that they may be saved through Christ for ever.

Any man who can hear such words as these without alarm must indeed be made of steel. And, if at times you feel such alarm at the prospect of what you are taking upon you, let me assure you, for your comfort, that that alarm will not diminish as you go forward. Progress in the work of the ministry is measured by an increasing sense of the terrifyingness of what we have to do, and our own utter incapacity to do it well. If you are inclined at times to think that a high theological degree, or personal charm, or a gift of eloquence will carry you through, I should regard that as a grave disqualification for the work of the ministry. If the call at times presents itself to you as unwelcome, if you are afraid as you look ahead, that in itself is no reason to suppose that you are not truly called. There is a craven fear that is unworthy of a true man and dishonoring to God. There is a godly fear, which is our continuing safeguard against the self-reliance that can blind us to our need of absolute

dependence upon God alone. Such fear I would regard
as the mark of the man who is truly called of God.

V *Qualities of a Minister*

Let us pass on to consider certain qualities which your
people have a right to expect to see in you, if your
ministry among them is to be effective.

I am not now referring to technical qualifications, such
as it is the purpose of your seminary training to provide.
The more of those you have the better; and three years
is all too short a time in which to acquire the elements of
them. I am concerned only with certain inner and spiritual qualifications, which, in my judgment, are essential
to any effective ministry.

The first is that we should ourselves be familiar with
the experience of the forgiveness of sins.

It would ill become me, speaking in a Lutheran Seminary, to expatiate on the doctrine of justification by faith.
In my experience, Lutherans always assume that no Episcopalian knows anything about justification by faith, and
if he does know anything, he knows it all wrong. Yet I
cannot pass by a matter which I judge to be crucial in
the sphere of vocation and ministry. We may differ as to
terms and precise theological definitions. The issue is
plainly set forth in the pages of the New Testament. "I
have been crucified with Christ; yet I live; and yet no
longer I, but Christ liveth in me: and that life which I
now live in the flesh I live in faith, the faith which is in
the Son of God who loved me and gave himself up for

me." In simpler words, Paul had learned that life can grow only out of death, hope only out of despair, power only out of the utter abandonment of self. God is not mocked; he will not give his glory to another; he can use only those men who have come to the point of claiming nothing for themselves.

People often speak of St. Paul as the classic example of a sudden conversion. I do not find myself in agreement with them. Certainly the experience on the Damascus road was sudden and very disturbing. The accompanying psychological shock is evident in what appears to have been paralysis of the retina and temporary blindness. But psychological shock is not the same as conversion. As I read the Scriptures, it seems that there had been a long period of preparation before, and that there was something of supreme importance that followed after. What followed was three days of blindness. Three days is a very long time, especially when you are blind and too much shaken even to eat.

What was Saul of Tarsus doing during those three days? I suppose that he was mostly fighting with ghosts. The ghosts of all those Christians whom he had hauled out of their houses and delivered up to prison and to death. The ghost of Stephen, who had been stoned to death outside the walls of Jerusalem, as Saul stood by and minded the clothes of those who stoned him. It is not fair that people should have the light of heaven on their faces, as they are being justly stoned to death; and in that process, it takes a terribly long time to die. Worst of all was the knowledge that he, Saul of Tarsus, had done all these things because he was resisting an inner conviction that he would not face. And I suppose that, as he meditated on all these things, he reached the conclusion that he could not be forgiven. Others perhaps but not Saul of Tarsus. Jesus of Nazareth had died that the mercy of God might be extended to all men, but not to Saul of Tarsus. Other men had sinned, but no other so desperately and willfully, so much against light and against his own inner truth. And so he is in the dark, helpless, undeserving and forsaken. And then, Ananias comes in, that unknown Ananaias, who appears once only on the stage of history, like that fellow-apprentice who won the young William Carey for Jesus Christ, and whose very name was forgotten for more than a hundred years. And Ananias is inspired to speak the perfect word: "Brother Saul." Shall man be greater than God? If the Christian, grievously wronged, can forgive, is it not certain that God also will forgive? In that simple word of human fellowship, the merciful compassion of the Saviour is brought home to him; he knows that even for Saul of Tarsus, the chief of sinners, his hands red with the blood of the saints, the death of Christ has availed, and he who was far off has now been brought nigh by the blood of Christ.

All Paul's teaching, even at its most abstract and theological, is determined by that experience of passing from death to life, from alienation to acceptance, from enmity to reconciliation, not for anything that he is in himself, not for anything that he has done, but solely through the illimitable goodness and compassion of God.

It is only through personal familiarity with that experience that we can venture to take on our lips the Gospel of the grace of God. In detail, the experience of Christian men is infinitely varied, since God deals with us as individuals and not as members of a race. In essentials, the experience of being crucified with Christ is always recognizably the same.

In our Episcopal Communion Service we say every Sunday, and indeed every day: "We are not worthy so much as to gather up the crumbs under the table; but thou art the same Lord whose property is always to have mercy." If we are sincere in our recognition of that unworthiness, then we take our stand on an equality in our penury. This is the foundation of the grand democracy of the Christian faith.

I was once traveling in India, when in the middle of the night two British soldiers burst in, and threw themselves down to sleep on the floor. By the morning, one of them had disappeared; the other had intelligently read the labels on my luggage and had discovered who I was. I do not think he had much idea of what a bishop might be, except that probably it was some kind of Christian; but at least he felt encouraged to make himself known to me. As we talked, through long hours, the outlines of his history began to emerge. He had been born in one of our seaport towns, had had very little education and no contact of any kind with the Church. He had been earning his living in the roughest work, loading trucks at the docks. Then came the war. In Palestine he had come in contact with the Salvation Army and had been converted. Of the reality of this experience there could be no possible doubt. With touching humility he explained to me in Salvation Army language that he was saved but not sanctified; and as I thought that that might serve fairly well as a description of me too, we found no difficulty in understanding each other. As we talked, differences of education, background, Church allegiance just faded away; there are moments at which the promise of the Lord, "where two or three are gathered together in my name, there am I in the midst of them," becomes almost tangible in its reality. I do not suppose that I shall ever see that man again; but perhaps we shall find each other out on the other side.

There are many ways of describing this experience; I would not wish to insist for a moment on any one terminology. But the experience itself is unmistakable. If you have come by that same way, and entered in through that same narrow door, you will have no difficulty in understanding what I am talking about. If you have not, it is no use pretending that some other experience will do as well. Much harm has been done by the distinction, popularized, though not invented by William James, between once-born Christians and twice-born Christians. When anyone tells me, as people sometimes do, that he is a once-born Christian, even though I may think that I know what he means, I can only feel sorry.

If this central experience is lacking, you may be able to do many admirable things in the work of the ministry. But one thing will be missing; I think the more sensitive among your people will feel that it is lacking. It is the proclamation of redemption through Christ, with the quiet authority of the man who knows by experience of what he speaks.

VI

Secondly I think that your people have the right to claim that, by your way of living before their eyes, you should make plain the nature of the guided life.

I use this word with a little hesitation. Clearly there is good biblical authority for its use: "I being in the way the Lord led me." But it happens that certain groups and fellowships have claimed a kind of monopoly of the term, and have used it in a way that has seemed to other Christians slightly ridiculous. In a sense, those groups had a right to regard themselves as having almost a proprietary right to the use of the term, since, for an uncounted number of Christians, they brought back to life an idea which ought to have been a normal part of Christian living, but which through disuse had remained very widely unknown. I well remember the headmaster of a big private school in England saying in a meeting: "It may seem strange to you, but although I had been a Christian for years, it had never occurred to me that, if I had a difficult letter to write, or a difficult interview with a parent in front of me, I could go down on my knees and ask for God's guidance, and expect that an answer would be given." It was only after his contact with the Oxford Group, as it was then called, that he found access to what was really part of his normal heritage as a Christian, but which he had never before known how to use. If there have been certain exaggerations in the developmentt of the idea of guidance, our right attitude is to reject neither the word nor the thing, but to restore both to their right proportions by relating them anew to the Bible doctrine of the Holy Spirit.

This morning I read, as in duty bound, the order for Morning Prayer according to the use of the Church of England, which every minister of our Church is pledged to read every day wherever he may be. There in the New Testament section for the day came the verse which has for many years been one of the cornerstones of my Christian faith: "The very hairs of your head are all numbered." If you take that saying of our Lord as true, you learn to live in one way; if you do not take it seriously, you live in a different way. Of course, there is the element of Oriental hyperbole in our Lord's utterance; I hope it may not be thought irreverent to suggest that God has more important things to do than literally numbering the hairs of our heads. But, if the words mean anything at all, they indicate that God is very seriously concerned with every part of our lives, and that we have a right to expect his help and guidance, even in matters that seem in themselves to be trifling. We must not descend to triviality; I suppose there is nothing to pre-

vent you as a Christian from asking guidance as to what
tie you should wear on a particular day, though I should
myself regard it as more sensible to trust your own judgment as to the color that will best match the suit you
are proposing to wear. But we have all had experience
in our lives of things that seemed very small, and yet
were fraught with consequences far beyond our power
to imagine at the time.

I think you may find that to take seriously the expectation of the guidance of God will produce something
like a revolution in the conduct of the affairs of your
Church.

Some time ago a missionary who is working in the
diocese of Lucknow described to me how things were
working out under the new bishop, who happens to be
a very old friend of mine. Probably by this time you
know well that church meetings are not always a scene
of unbroken harmony and concord; the old Adam and
the old serpent can find plenty of space to stretch themselves, and the result may be weariness and frustration
for those who take part. "But," said my informant, "under the new bishop, a day of diocesan meetings is much
more like a quiet day for prayer than anything else. If
ever the business shows signs of getting entangled, or
the way through is not clearly seen, the bishop says,
'Well now, we'd better spend a little time in prayer.'
So the whole council gets down on its knees and waits
to see whether God has anything to say on that particular point." I am afraid that that is rather a contrast

to most of our Church meetings. Usually we start with a short prayer *pro forma* at the beginning; then the field is opened to the rival views and opinions of men; the still small voice of the Spirit is not easily discerned and sometimes it may be that what God really intends is very different from the wisdom of man's devising.

In our individual lives, we must keep our sense of humor, and not expect God to be always interposing directly in our affairs. I was once driving out to the airport at San Francisco, which is a considerable way from the city, when we got involved in the traffic stream going to a football game, and it became more evident every moment that we were not going to reach the airport in time. The young clergyman who was kindly driving me remarked that he had friends in the Oxford Group who believed that everything in our lives was providentially ordered for good. I could only answer that in a long experience of misfortunes in travel, I had on many occasions been unable to detect any purpose in the way things had worked out—other, of course, than the sanctification of the traveler. (Lest you should feel too sympathetic, I should add that on that occasion I did, wholly unexpectedly, catch my plane!) And yet, I do try to live up to my beliefs. I try never to start on a journey without praying that it may be useful to someone. I was not certain what forces had been at work when once a Turkish gentleman leaned across in the train, and asked me to explain in French the significance of predestination in the Christian faith! But how often has the apparently chance contact in a railway car been found to have far more than a transitory significance.

VII

The third quality grows directly out of the second, but is distinct from it. Your people have the right to expect that you will manifest the grace of *Ataraxia*. I apologize for using the Greek word, but it is beautifully expressive and to the point; it is the life that is free from strain and worry and anxiety. It is our Lord's own word in John 14: *Mē tarachtheto hē kardiā humōn.* "Let not your heart be troubled." In another very familiar passage he tells us that we are to take no anxious thought for tomorrow. At this point, the King James version, "Take no thought for the morrow," tends to be misleading. If you take no thought for the morrow, you certainly will not pass your examinations. Take no *anxious* thought. Do not try to do tomorrow's work today. God gives daily bread for one day only; if you try today to do tomorrow's work without his grace, you cannot complain if that double burden breaks you.

Worry is the great disease of our Western civilisation. That is a plain physical fact. Modern research is steadily extending the range of those diseases which are classed as psychosomatic, in which the element of mental strain plays at least as important a part as the physical symptom. We are destroying ourselves by our anxieties. The most characteristic buildings in a modern city are the gigantic hospitals. Having produced a civilization which with the utmost ingenuity tears men in pieces, we then expend countless dollars and almost divine ingenuity in somehow piecing them together again.

It is very hard for Christians to take seriously the doctrine of Jesus that worry is sin. We have come so much to take it for granted that we have lost the sense that it is contrary to the will of God. I have known students who were so used to worrying that, if for a moment they stopped, they began immediately to worry again with a guilty conscience over the vacuum that had been left inside them by the worry when it stopped.

I suppose ministers are about the most worried class of people in the world. If you take it on the human plane, they have every reason to be so. Next Sunday's sermon begins to loom above the horizon almost as soon as last Sunday's has sunk below it; it is only human to be a little perturbed as to whether it will be as good as the last, and up to the standard that your people have come to expect from you. No church is wholly free from divisions and from the strivings of men. Deacons and elders and vestries can be to the minister highly afflictive bodies. Most of you will be called to live and keep up appearances on a salary on which your lay brethren would regard it as ridiculous to be expected to make both ends meet. Undoubtedly on the human plane there is every ground for worry. But you are not called to live on the human plane; you are called to live in the world of faith, where worry is judged as sin.

You will find, I think, that worry is almost always

concerned with an error about time or place, wanting to be somewhere else, or wanting to be in some time other than the present. The student who is worrying about an examination three weeks ahead is really trying to write the examination answers now, which, as he has not the questions before him, is a rather difficult thing to do. No wonder that he is worried. The minister who is fretting over his sermon at night is really trying to preach his sermon in bed, an unprofitable occupation in the absence of the congregation. A man who is worrying about the health of a distant relative is in fact often saying unconsciously, "I ought to be there and doing something about it, and I can't because I'm here." "There" and "then" are the hallmarks of worry. "Here" and "now" are the only places in which to learn the lessons of trust and Christian health.

God's co-ordinates run inexorably along the lines of here and now; and those meet always at one particular point, at which and at no other God is able to meet you. The Augustana Seminary, Rock Island, Illinois, Jan. 5th morning 1950; at the moment, this is the only place in all the world where God is able to make himself accessible to you. But if you are prepared to live always by the rule of *here and now* you will find that God can prove his adequacy to every need.

There is a story in the life of Hudson Taylor, the founder of the China Inland Mission, which has often helped me. On one occasion, while he was talking to a young member of the mission, letters came in bringing news of serious rioting in two stations of the mission, and of grave danger to the life of the missionaries. George Nichol was about to slip out, and leave Mr. Taylor alone, when to his astonishment he heard someone begin to whistle. Turning back, he said with some indignation, "How can you whistle when our friends are in such danger?" "Would you have me anxious and troubled?" was Taylor's quiet reply. "That would not help them, and would certainly incapacitate me for my work. I have just to roll the burden on the Lord." What he had been whistling was the refrain of the old hymn, "Jesus, I am resting, resting, In the joy of what thou art."

Rolling off the burden on him. "Casting all your care up on him, for he careth for you." Do you know the exact translation of that? "Rolling off all your worries on him, and he will do the worrying for you." I have always liked the story which I read in Dr. Fosdick's book, *On Being a Real Person*, about the bishop who, deeply troubled about the affairs of his diocese and praying far into the night, heard God say to him almost audibly, "Quayle, you go to bed, I'll sit up the rest of the night."

Live here and now. Recollect always that underneath are the everlasting arms, here and now. Do what you can. Those are the three rules for effectiveness in the ministry or indeed in any form of Christian living. Do what you can. In my experience God deals wonderfully gently with the honest mistakes, such as all of us are likely to make, and guards our people from being harmed by them. He does not give any guarantee that we shall be

3 rules for effectiveness

always right; he does promise that when we are honest and humble, he will be with us in the way.

Perhaps you have guessed why I have laid such stress on *Ataraxia*. Most of you must have seen that very remarkable photograph which appeared in *Life* magazine some time ago, of people on a New York street corner; very ordinary people, taken on no special occasion, and on almost every face you can see the marks of frustration, anxiety or fear. It is very strange that it should be so, in the richest and most powerful country that the world has ever known. But so it is. As you look down from the pulpit on your people, you will often see that unmistakable expression; and you must remember that you cannot heal your people, unless you yourself have been healed.

VIII

You will see that each of the three special qualities I have required in the minister is concerned with peace. There is first the peace of the man who knows that by the grace of Christ his sins are forgiven. "Therefore being justified by faith, we have peace with God through Jesus Christ our Lord." Then there is the peace of the man who knows that his way is ordered by one wiser than himself, and has experienced the truth of the promise, "Thine ears shall hear a word behind thee saying, This is the way, walk ye in it; when ye turn to the right hand and when ye turn to the left." There is the peace of the man who has learned to cast his burdens on the Lord, and not to carry more than is appointed for him and proportioned to his strength.

Remember that in the Bible peace is no negative thing; it is not the mere absence of war; much less is it an escapist formula. God's peace is participation in the triumph which comes when God's will is really being done.

There is a special blessing in the Gospel on the peacemakers. I think that this may be extended to the peacebringers. You cannot bring peace to your people unless you have yourself known the peace of God that passeth understanding. If you can both live in it, and tell of it, and manifest it, those to whom you bring it as a gift will rise up and call you blessed.

❧ 3 ❧

The Minister and His Message

I

"I SHRANK not from declaring unto you the whole counsel of God." This claim of St. Paul in his speech to the elders of the Church of Ephesus might seem to have in it a trace of arrogance. Yet, if you read through the ten letters which can be most certainly ascribed to him, and which can be read right through slowly in four hours, you will find that St. Paul is not boasting, but simply stating a fact. There are happily many different lights and insights in the New Testament; but there is no single theological topic of importance which is not at some point or other taken up by St. Paul, and illuminated briefly and vividly by his words.

If you enter upon the ordained life, what will be committed to you will be precisely the same responsibility; you will be charged with declaring to your people the whole counsel of God.

I am always glad that I belong to a Church which observes the liturgical order of the Christian year, since this ensures that I must preach at least once a year on the main theological topics of our faith. I am afraid that if this were not so, I should not often be found preaching on the doctrine of the Ascension or that of the Trinity. But Ascension Day and Trinity Sunday remorselessly come round; and, if I am in the pulpit on those days, I must do my best with those difficult doctrines.

Some of you belong to churches which do not keep the Christian year, though I note with interest how rapidly the observance of at least some parts of it is spreading even in the least liturgical of churches. If you have not this check and safeguard, it is most important that you should devise others of your own. I hope that you will keep a record of your sermons. And you may perhaps take it as a part of that solemn self-examination which we ought to put ourselves through on the last evening of the year, to look back over the past year, and to see what you really have been talking about. If you found that of your texts for the year, 40 per cent were drawn from the Gospels, 25 per cent from the rest of the New Testament, 25 per cent from the Old Testament, you might feel that you had been reasonably faithful to your obligation. You will note that that leaves you five or six Sundays in the year, but no more, to preach on special topics, without necessarily taking a text from the Scriptures. In such a matter, there are no rules, only certain principles. But, if in your self-examination you found that you had departed very far from my rough estimate of obligations, you might do well to consider carefully whether in your preaching you were honestly preserving the *proportion* of the faith, or whether your own predilections had played an undue part in your choice of themes.

Having said this, and recognizing that there is a vast range and variety of topics on which at one time or another you may rightly preach, I come back to remind you that there is one central theme and one only, which you are authorized and accredited to preach. We are appointed to preach Christ, and him only.

It sometimes happens that we preach well, but that the one thing needful is missing. An eminent Methodist in England, whose work involves a great deal of traveling, told me that often when he returns home on Monday he asks his wife about the sermon she had heard the day before, and that not infrequently the answer is, "Unitarian sermon again." The thoroughly orthodox Methodist brethren who had preached these sermons would no doubt be horrified if told that they had been setting forth unitarian doctrine. Yet unless we are watchful, we can so easily slip into preaching morals, or history or philosophy, or a general theism—anything, in fact, except the Gospel of the grace of God in Jesus Christ. Another friend described to me a sermon he had heard in a church not a thousand miles from here. It is a great church, with a fine congregation. On that day, the church was packed and the people hung in rapt attention on the words of the preacher, as he delivered a fine and eloquent sermon. But it was all about uplift and progress, and the American way of life, with not a word about the Lordship of

Jesus Christ or redemption through him. That is a trick which can very easily be learned. If you have any gift for eloquence, in a few years' time you too can have congregations hanging on your words as you discourse on the American way of life. But if you preach that kind of stuff, what you will be giving your people is just what Tennyson in *In Memoriam* rather bitterly called "vacant chaff well-meant for grain."

In the earlier years of the nineteenth century the most influential pulpit in the world was that of Holy Trinity Church, Cambridge, where for more than fifty years the great Charles Simeon held forth Sunday by Sunday. (A little girl taken to hear him clutched her mother's arm and said, "Mamma, what is the gentleman in a passion about?") Across the desk in that pulpit, there is a slip of paper, on which is written, "Sir, we would see Jesus." You might do worse than put such a slip of paper in your own pulpit, to remind you what you are there for. What people want is not our scholarship, though, if we have any, that is a good gift that can be used. It is not our eloquence, though that also can be used, if kept under stern control. It is not our personality, though, try as we will, we cannot wholly eliminate that from our work. What they need is to see Jesus. Unless you are lifting him up, unless people come out of your church Sunday by Sunday saying, "We have seen the living Christ," your ministry is not a ministry of the Gospel.

After all the American public does not know Christ. They have heard of him, and have some strange ideas about him. But for the most part they have not met *him*. What America needs perhaps more than anything else is to be delivered from the vague sentimental images of Jesus that many of its people have retained from hymns sung in Sunday school as children, and to meet the real Christ in the terror of his judgments and in his living power.

II

There is always a danger that the preacher may present to the imagination of his people no more than the fruits of his own imagination. From this danger you will be saved, if you fulfill your ministry rightly by the fact that you will be commissioned as a minister of *the Word*.

Those who talk most about the word of God are not always, as I have observed, those who are most diligent in reading it. But, in fact, you cannot really be a preacher of the Word, unless you are so diligent in the study of the Scriptures that they become part of your very being, and condition both the way in which you think and the way in which you speak.

If you look back over the history of the Church, you will find that all the greatest preachers have been men whose minds were steeped in the words of Scripture. Of Origen, the greatest scholar of the early Church, Bishop Westcott has remarked somewhere that he seems to have held the whole of Scripture in solution in his mind. Of St. John Chrysostom I read not long ago that in those great folio volumes of his sermons, which I cannot claim to have read *in extenso*, there are seven thousand quotations from the Old Testament, and eleven thousand from the New. Slight variations from the standard text of the Scriptures show that those great men generally quoted from memory; their minds were so full of Scripture that the words came naturally, and both thought and expression formed themselves according to the Scriptural pattern. I think you can always tell, listening to a preacher, whether he is a man of the Word or not, whether, that is to say, apart from quoting the Bible, he is really thinking biblically, with a mind controlled and fashioned by biblical categories and points of view. If we are men of the Word, we have the fullest liberty to let our minds and our imagination work on the material before us; but we are safe from the undue subjectivism which always ends by distorting the message.

We are to be men of the Bible and of the whole Bible. Again I am thankful for the liturgical order of my Church, which requires that we read through the greater part of the Old Testament once a year, and the whole of the New Testament twice a year. I cannot say that I always find the daily lessons specially inspiring and appropriate; but I am sure that the principle of consecutive reading is sound. If your Church does not provide you with such a steady discipline of Bible-reading, it is essential that you should provide it for yourself, on any system that you like, provided that it really is a system, and that it really covers the ground. Naturally we shall devote more time to the New Testament than to the Old and even in the New Testament there will be some parts that will require closer attention than others. But unless we correct the intensive approach by some system of more comprehensive study, we shall run the danger of becoming dangerously selective, and of limiting ourselves and therefore our people, to only a small part of the great biblical highway.

From time to time, people produce shortened Bibles. It is curious to note how unsatisfactory these always are, and how they always omit something which a reader has particularly wanted to use. A general in the British Army told me that, at the crisis of the North African campaign, he wanted to read to his troops the passage in Ephesians about the whole armor of God. All that he had with him was a book called something like "The Bible arranged to be read as literature." When he turned it up, he found that in this book the whole Epistle to the Ephesians had been omitted, on the ground presumably that Colossians would do just as well. This is an extreme case. I would not go to the other extreme and suggest that you will gain great spiritual benefit from meditation on a page of the names in the first book of Chronicles. But, if you omit any large section of Scripture, you are certain to lose something of value. Gems are scattered about the Scriptures in considerable profusion, and are likely to turn up in unexpected places. You may not be very familiar with the book of Lamentations; but, if you will take a quarter of an hour off to read it, you will find that it contains some of the finest sayings in the whole of the Old Testament.

III

We are to preach the Word of God. But where do we begin?

It may console you to know that even the best preachers and the most experienced ministers sometimes find that, when they contemplate the prospect of preaching next Sunday, their mind becomes a perfect blank. This is much more likely to happen to you in the early days of your ministry. You seem to have said all you know on every subject you know anything about. As the days pass, your mind becomes, if anything, blanker than before, and the very tension of anxiety makes it unlikely that you will find a good solution of the problem. In teaching students of my own Church, I have always reminded them that in such a situation there is a ready way out of the difficulty. For each Sunday there are the appointed readings from the Epistles and from the Gospels. Start on Monday, and honestly meditate for half an hour a day on the appointed passage. You will find by the end of the week that you have something to say to your people. It may not be great preaching; it may not be one of your best efforts; but it will be recognizably the Word of God. If you have no liturgical tradition to guide you, take almost any passage from the Gospels or Epistles, follow the same method, and you will find that something worth while comes out of it.

You must not, of course, suppose from what I have just said that turning to the Word of God is the last resort in an otherwise desperate situation. This is merely one application of what ought to be a general principle. Our usual practice ought to be to preach from texts rather than on subjects. One of the greatest defects in the contemporary pulpit is the lack of straightforward expository preaching. We all tend to overestimate our people's acquaintance with Scripture. On the whole, they are very ignorant of it. They do not know what is in the Bible; they find its language perplexing; their minds are not attuned to its categories of thought. And yet they want to know what is in it; they are aware that it is a great demesne, of which they have not yet acquired the freedom, and are remarkably grateful to anyone who will supply the key. Wherever there is a return to honest biblical exposition from the pulpit, there seems to be immediate response in the pew.

William Temple, when rector of a church in London, once preached steadily through the Gospel of St. John, omitting nothing. It took him about four years to get through. The fruits of that long labor of thought and preparation were seen when many years later he wrote down his famous *Readings in St. John's Gospel*. At present you would be well-advised not to attempt anything on so grandiose a scale. But, if you will make it a regular habit to take not an isolated text but a passage of Scripture up to ten verses in length, seriously and steadily expound it, say what it has meant to you as you have

pondered it in preparation for your sermon, show its
relevance to your people as they listen, and let that
biblical material, drop by drop, make its way into your
hearers' minds, I think you will find that they recognize
that you are doing one of the most important things
that can be done by the preacher as he stands in the
pulpit with the Word of God before him.

IV

All strong preaching has intellectual fiber, both in its
construction and in its appeal. But do not take me to
mean that the primary end of preaching is instruction,
and that its primary excellence is intellectual. Preaching
is aimed at the whole man. It cannot be fully effective,
unless it is delivered under a strong sense of urgency,
and directed toward personal decision. A friend said to
me not long ago that he listened to many sermons, but
only rarely felt in them that sense of urgency, the feeling that something has to be done about all this, and
that people must make up their minds.

The report of the second section at the Amsterdam
Assembly of the World Council of Churches, a rather
sober document, at one point comes to life in the words,
"If the Gospel really is a matter of life and death . . ."
Do you regard the Gospel as a matter of life and death?
If not, you have no business to think of being a min-
ister. But, if you do, surely that belief must impress a
special character on every act of your ministry.

I am not suggesting that every sermon should convey

a direct appeal in words, still less that that appeal should be accompanied by emotion. In some denominations, the appeal for conversion has in the past been made so frequently, and perhaps in such a bullying way, that now it has ceased to have any effect at all, and many younger preachers, even in those denominations, have reacted rather strongly against the presentation of any personal challenge. There is perhaps a tendency in American preaching toward an overemphasis, which results in nothing being really emphatic, just as in much English preaching there is such a studious avoidance of every kind of emphasis that it is sometimes hard to believe that it can all be about anything at all important after all.

But is there not a middle way between the overintellectual and the overemotional, in the recognition that preaching should be directed above all else to the will? Were not our forefathers right in saying that we should preach as dying men to dying men? To harp on the thought of death would be morbid. But surely it is only common sense to recognize that we all are mortal, and that any one of us at any moment may be called to render up his account. I hope that I shall be here tomorrow to give the next talk in this series. But after all, I have no certainty. We hope that all of you will be here tomorrow to hear me. Yet it may be that one of you is listening to the Gospel for the last time. That being so, can I possibly occupy myself with trivialities? Shall I not wish that my words should bear some relation to the grace of our Lord Jesus Christ and the love of God and the fellowship of the Holy Spirit? Somehow the note of urgency, of decision, of the issues of life and death must come back into our preaching.

It would be a great mistake to try to bring it back artificially by some process of emotional strain. I believe that it will come back quietly, unemotionally and naturally, if you are prepared day by day to sit at the foot of the Cross and learn of the Crucified. After all, most of your time you will be surrounded by men and women, who, though redeemed by Christ, are still outside the circle of redemption. If that is not an urgent situation, what is?

V

But if so many men and women, and this is the fact, are outside, how can we ever speak to them? How can we bring our message into a form in which it is felt to be relevant to modern man in his contemporary needs and pressures?

A good many years ago a friend of mine who is a strong Anglo-Catholic said to me, "I couldn't preach, if I wasn't hearing confessions." Most of you belong to denominations in which the practice of formal confession to God in the presence of the minister is not observed, and you may be slightly shocked by his remark. But it is clear what he meant. In dealing intimately with people as individuals, in discovering their real needs and problems and failings, he was discovering what preaching was really for. I would myself express that rather differently: "I could not preach, unless I was constantly in touch with people." I have never in my life found any course of addresses more difficult to prepare than the ones from which this book is written, because I was honest enough to admit to myself that really I knew nothing about American seminary students and their needs. Now I know a little more than I did.

You see, preaching is like weaving. There are the two factors of the warp and the woof. There is the fixed, unalterable element, which for us is the Word of God; there is the variable element, which enables the weaver to change and vary the pattern at his will. For us that variable element is the constantly changing pattern of people and of situations. How wide that variety is, you will realize if you read the great sermons of the past. Red-hot and effective in their day, there is hardly one of them that would not leave the congregation cold today. But that is not surprising. Once at Hartlebury Castle, the ancient palace of the bishops of Worcester, I had the privilege of sleeping in a bed the blankets for which had been woven in the eighteenth century; very interesting and historic, but on the whole I prefer to sleep under twentieth century Witney!

There is no point on which I wish to insist with greater force than this—that you should allow your preaching to grow out of your daily contacts with your flock. And by that word "flock," I do not mean the docile sheep which are already feeding in your enclosed pastures; I include all those who are still outside, and whom you earnestly hope to win. Welcome every opportunity of contact with them. Remember that the fault of most preachers is that they talk too much and do not listen. Wherever you are, in the train, on the streetcar, in the drugstore, take every opportunity of conversation, and above all do your share of the listening. Try to find what people are thinking about and what they are interested in. Above all, find out, if it comes naturally, what they think about the Christian faith, and under what strange illusions as to its nature they suffer.

Very often, the ideas of people are very different from what we imagine. Even with our own Church people, it is sometimes humiliating to discover that we have assumed far too much, and that there are blocks of skepticism or misunderstanding in their minds which are neutralizing for them the positive content of our teaching.

Let me give one illustration. A year or two ago, it was laid down by the authorities of the British Army of Occupation in Germany that officers were to be put through courses in "Moral Leadership," which meant in fact courses of instruction in the Christian faith; so all kinds of generals and high-ranking officers found themselves back at school, faced by perhaps the first opportunity since they were actually at school to think out their own attitude to the faith, and to put plain questions to experts. During one of the discussions, a highly placed officer put this question: "Can we really put much reliance on the Gospels, if the first of them was not written earlier than the fourth century A.D.?" This was a genuine and sincere question. You can easily understand what had happened. Some time or another, probably at the time when the British people were paying £100,000 to buy the Codex Sinaiticus from the Russians, this good man had read in the papers that the earliest *manuscript* of the New Testament we possess was written in the fourth century (even so, he was rather out of date, and apparently had not heard of the discovery of the Chester Beatty papyrus); and not unnaturally had confused the date of the earliest existing manuscript with that of the composition of the books themselves. Now if a man is suffering from a fundamental skepticism of that kind, it is certain that he will put a question mark after every sentence of your exposition of the beauties of St. John.

It is my experience that such doubts are much more common even among churchgoing laymen than we often suppose. One of the best pieces of apologetic work I have ever been able to do was on a crowded troop ship coming home from India. Being in rather bad health, I refused to organize a discussion group, but I said that I should be pleased to run it, if any of the officers cared to get it going. The three brigadiers on board got busy, and before long we had running a splendid and entirely informal discussion group on deck, attended by anything between fifteen and thirty officers. By the end of the voyage we had to meet everyday because the number of questions coming in was so large. I insisted on written questions, in order to encourage serious and definite inquiry. I remember that one of the questions was on this very point of the reliability of the Gospels: How far are the Gospels trustworthy as historical evidence? To what extent can they be checked from other sources? How much do we really know of the life and words of Christ? Without any books at all available I did my best to clear up the matter for them. What was interesting was that, after I had given a rather long answer, and there had been some supplementary questions, the Irish officer who had put the original question said, "Why don't the clergy tell us this kind of thing from the pulpit?"

It would be a great mistake to take much of your limited time in the pulpit for the discussion of historical or critical questions. The right place for such problems is the discussion group or the Bible course. But you will never get people into discussion groups, unless they discover from your attitude in the pulpit that you welcome honest questions, however unorthodox, and that you are willing to be interested in the problems that perplex them; and unless they gather that you have sufficient intellectual guns to be able to give them satisfaction on their own intellectual level. Such apologetic work is never more than a preliminary to the preaching of the Gospel; but it can be quite an important preliminary, especially in these days of secular education and innumerable anti-Christian influences.

VI

If there are problems of intellectual preconception, there are also problems of sheer unfamiliarity with biblical language and biblical ways of thinking. Even if we have begun to understand the needs and perplexities of people, how can we get our message across to them in ways that they will really understand? The important thing is not what we say in the pulpit, but what people understand of what we say, and above all, what they remember. This is a much more serious matter than most ministers are willing to realize. We almost all slip into the use of a "dialect of Canaan" which, congenial to the established Christian, rarely makes contact with the mind of the beginner or the stranger.

When a young man complained to me of the unfamiliarity of the language of the pulpit, I asked him to give examples. His reply was, "Well, they use words like *Grace*." They do! I would not suggest that you develop such a use of the vernacular as, for instance, that of the late Billy Sunday; but we should never be too proud to learn from others, even when we cannot precisely imitate them.

The first principle to be borne in mind is that in preaching, simplicity is a grace greatly to be desired, but that for most of us it comes only by hard labor. One of my brothers was for many years on the staff of a famous school in West Africa. Although a layman, he developed a considerable gift for preaching. I found that it was his habit to write out his sermons twice; after the first writing, he would go through and take out every word which an African boy of fourteen, listening to a sermon in English, could not be expected readily to understand. You are not likely to have to put yourself through as severe a discipline as that.

Do not suppose that simplicity of speech necessarily involves superficiality of thought. Look at the Gospels in the King James version, and you will find that our Lord's deepest teaching is set forth almost entirely in plain, strong Anglo-Saxon words of one syllable. (As an awful warning, contrast the first and second sentences of this paragraph.)

I may add an example, of which I have already made use in print. A clergyman in England, who knew that he was not a very good preacher, was asked in middle age to become the rector of a country parish. This was a new type of work to him; and in order to make his ministry effective, he decided not to use any word in his preaching unless he had first heard it on the lips of a member of his parish. As he talked with the people, he noted down the words they used, and eventually had a vocabulary of about three hundred words. That may seem to you a very small number; but investigation shows that the number of words people actually use is surprisingly small, though most people understand a good many more words than they use themselves. So this country clergyman, having got his rural vocabulary, limited himself to it, and found a way to set out his teaching in

those familiar terms. The result was that before long not
merely was his church full, but the churchyard was full
too, with people who had come to hear the parson "who
talked sense in the pulpit." If you were to receive that
commendation from your people, you would not be doing too badly.

If that were the whole problem of communication,
our task would not be too difficult. Unfortunately, there
is far more to it than that. Words are not dead things,
with just so much meaning and no more. They have
overtones and undertones, and the power to set bells of
emotion and imagination ringing in men's minds.

As we were reminded last night, in the days of the
great campaigns of D. L. Moody, the Christian words
were still familiar to men, and carried with them a certain
amount of emotional significance. The skill of the evan-
gelist lay in working on that half-conscious emotion, until it came into the field of consciousness, and a definite
Yes or No was demanded of the hearer. There is a
worthy as well as an unworthy use of emotion. Now,
except among people brought up to the Church, we cannot count on any such reverberation of the Christian
words. Take the word "heaven." "Heaven, heaven, Going to shout all about God's heaven." You and I can feel
in that something of the immense faith and hope of the
Negro, that faith and hope that gilded with a certain
splendor his drab and sorrowful days. Think what the
Marxists have made of that; clearly an escapist symbol,
devised by the possessing classes for the better quieting

of their own consciences and the better enslavement of
the poor!

How are we to find the language that sets the right
bells ringing in the minds of men today? Our Lord did
it by the use of parables. In some fields of work, we can
make those parables live again today. In a very poor little
congregation in India, sitting among the oppressed out-
castes, I have seen the eyes of ignorant old women light
up, as I expounded the Parable of the Sower; that was
something that they knew, and had seen at work all
around them in their own fields. But what are the parables that are effective in the rundown areas of our great
cities, in a world the intellectual horizon of which is
bounded by the race tracks, the movies and the comic
strips? Do not think for a moment that I am decrying
the fold who live in those areas; you will find among
them just as magnificent human material as anywhere
else in the world. But it is just the fact that among them
the imagination has been starved and atrophied. The best
that our boasted civilization has been able to do has been
to produce a race of men, who in the field of imagination
and creative activity are pygmies. The poverty of their
inner life conditions their capacity for response to religious impressions.

What are the parables and images that will set in movement the right reverberations in the minds of the mass
of our people today? I am afraid the answer is that none
of us knows. And it is urgent that we should know. The
right use of the imagination plays an immensely im-

portant part in religious thought and experience. We
have only to turn once again to the prophets of Israel to
see that that is so. I doubt whether there has ever been
a writer in any language who has possessed in a higher
degree than the prophet Isaiah that intensity of imagination through which words become molten in the mind
of the user, and flow into new channels that he has devised for them. What we call "touching the heart" is
often an inaccurate expression for "kindling the imagination." How that is to be done in the modern world is
an almost unsolved problem; here you have open before
you an almost unlimited field for your practical experi-
mentation and research.

VII

Perhaps we have dwelt too long on methods and techniques. *How* you preach is important, but *what* you
preach is very much more important still. And what you
are commissioned to preach is the Gospel.

Wherever the Gospel is truly preached, it brings divi-
sion. It was so in the days of Jesus of Nazareth; what
brought joy to some kindled fury and hatred in the
hearts of others. This is because the Gospel is always
two-edged. It is both life and death, both judgment and
mercy; it is both the message which men love to hear,
and the message which men hate to hear. It never can
be otherwise. You must take account in your ministry of
this dual aspect of that which you proclaim.

First, it is the message which men love to hear. The

Gospel came to the world as good news—good news for those who were not hearing good news from anywhere else. "Come unto me all ye that labor and are heavy laden, and I will give you rest." There are plenty of people in the world who still need that message; whether it is the Indian woman carrying her heavy waterpot daily half a mile to the well, because in most of the 750,000 villages of India there are still no pumps and no water supply in the houses; or the operative in a great factory here, worn out by the sheer monotony of his job, anxious as to when he will be able to get married, and where he will be able to find a home when he does; or the poor minister, drained of vitality by the frustrations of his job and the imperfect sympathy of his people.

"I will give you rest." This message is not to be proclaimed sentimentally, as though it could provide an escape from the hardness of life. You will find that sentiment does not go down well in the docks and the prison and the concentration camp. It is to be proclaimed as the message of joy that gives men mastery over circumstances, even when circumstances are at their worst, and the power to live again. It is not to be proclaimed as a substitute for social action, but as, what in fact it is, the one power which makes social action possible in an otherwise unredeemable community. If you can honestly proclaim the message as the word which has brought you rest, some at least will respond and say, "Yes, this *is* good news; this is what we need."

But remember also that the Gospel is the message

which men hate to hear. Because the Gospel brings the judgment of God, there is something in every one of us which is naturally and inveterately rebellious against it. Much of what you have to tell men is just what they most hate to hear.

You are commissioned to tell them that the wages of sin is death.

We are living in days of deep uneasiness about our civilization. Our Russian friends tell us very plainly that our civilization is dying, and that in trying to keep it going, we are merely propping up a simulacrum from the past. Many of our own prophets also tell us, in accents of mournful gloom, or of hardly concealed jubilation, that it is dying. We are sometimes tempted to wonder ourselves. If it is dying, that can only be because the wages of sin is death. If, though still vital, it is racked by contradictions, tensions and conflicts, that again can only be because the wages of sin is death.

We try to evade this plain biblical issue. There has been a lot of loose talk in recent years about the tyranny of the machine. "Machines are in the saddle and ride mankind," I seem to remember someone saying. Poor machines! Why should they be made the scapegoats for our follies and abominations? What is true is that the application of mechanical power to industry did greatly increase man's power over man, and that for the most part that increased power fell in early days into the hands of robber barons—wicked, unscrupulous, selfish men, who cared for themselves, but were not at all grieved for the affliction of Joseph. If we are being destroyed, our destruction comes of ourselves and not from anywhere else.

Some people speak of demonic forces at work in the world, and of the power that they acquire over nations and men. I think that quite probably that is true; St. Paul was using more than a metaphor when he spoke of wrestling against principalities and powers and the rulers of the darkness of this world. But who gave these demonic powers the privilege of entrance into the affairs of men? They can do nothing against us, unless, like Faust, we fail to close one corner of the pentacle, and so give them access to our sanctuary. And so again, if we are being destroyed, our destruction cometh of ourselves.

Many today have fallen under the spell of the myth of the sinless proletariat. All iniquity must be attributed to the capitalist and the exploiter and none to his victim. As Christians, we may not subscribe to this myth. I, for one, have immense admiration for the so-called working class. But it is impossible to know that class, even a little, and to imagine the members of it to be sinless. To them, no less than to the exploiter, we are charged to bring the message that the wages of sin is death, and that, if we are being destroyed, our destruction cometh of ourselves. They will not like the message very much either.

The pillars of the world are justice, righteousness and truth; and these, like the Gospel, or rather, because they are part of the Gospel, are twofold in their action. To the man who tries to guide his life according to them, they are a principle of life and health. But when they are infringed, they are ruthless in their counteraction as judgment and destruction.

Try to preach faithfully this Gospel both of judgment and of mercy, and see what happens.

Inevitably the faithful preacher of the Gospel will shock the complacency of his hearers. But let us remind ourselves that we are not authorized ever to give unnecessary pain. We must aim to speak the truth; we must never aim to wound. The feelings of our hearers must be as sacred to us as our own.

We all know, for instance, that there is a modern view of the Bible. The great achievement of New Testament criticism is that it has brought us nearer to the Man Jesus of Nazareth than any generation since the Canon of the New Testament was closed. It is the triumph of Old Testament criticism that we are able to read the messages of the prophets with new eyes, in relation to the situation in which they were first spoken. It is good that our congregations should be enabled to share these good things with us. As scribes instructed unto the kingdom of heaven, you should bring forth from your treasures things new as well as old. But I have known pert young ministers fresh from seminary bring forth new things in such a way as to cause the utmost distress to faithful Christians, who were living by the Word of God long before the minister was born. After all, we are not saved by knowing that Isaiah 53 was almost certainly not written by Isaiah; and it may well be that the deaf old granny in the front row knows more than you will ever understand of what it means that the Lord hath laid on him the iniquity of us all.

In my own Church, there is considerable variety of liturgical practice. I have known young ministers come to a new parish, and introduce changes with such brutal lack of consideration for the feelings of their people, that many of the worshipers in perplexity and distress have ceased altogether to come to church, or have gone off to the Methodist church around the corner!

If you do such things, you will be deservedly unpopular, and you will not have the sympathy of any right-minded people. And, further, you will be under the judgment and condemnation of God, who has charged you to feed and not to harry his people.

But when all is said and done, there is, as Kierkegaard was never weary of reminding us, "the offence of the Cross." Jesus of Nazareth is an offence and a scandal, and can never be anything else. If you are appointed to a rather rich and comfortable church, try preaching, when the right moment has come, on James V, "Go to now, ye rich men, weep and howl for your miseries that are coming upon you." Make as clear as you can the teaching of the Epistle, and see what happens. You may find that the following Sunday there are empty places in the seats of the mighty where the rich men were wont to sit. If so, do not be unduly discouraged.

When I urged you to be closely in touch with your people, to be sensitive to their needs and to treat their feelings with reverence, I did not mean that you were to make yourself subject to their judgment. "With me it is a very small thing that I should be judged of you, or of man's judgment," writes St. Paul to the Corinthians. Write out those words, put them at the top of your desk, and look at them as you prepare your sermon. Your judgment is with the Lord and your recompense with your God. Whether they will hear or whether they will forbear, you must proclaim his Word as he gave it to you, and you have understood it.

If the result is that you start by emptying your church, do not be unduly dismayed. You will after all be in good company. In the sixth chapter of St. John's Gospel, we read that, when our Lord began to give deep teaching about eating his flesh and drinking his blood, many of his hearers said, "This is a hard saying," and walked no more with him. The Greek word does not mean "difficult to understand"; it means "shocking." Such things ought not to be said in respectable pulpits! And so they turned away. Our Lord then asks the disciples "Will ye also go away?" That, I am sure, is to be taken as a real question—"you can go away, if you want to." And you know Peter's answer, "Lord, to whom shall we go? Thou hast the words of eternal life." If you faithfully preach the offense of the Cross, it is certain that some will find the way too difficult, and will leave you. But they may come back. If it can in any measure be truly said of you, "Thou hast the words of eternal life," you will never lack for hearers, though at times they may be few.

And, if you do not intend to proclaim the words of eternal life, do not attempt to preach at all.

✠ 4 ✠

The Minister and His People

I

IT IS interesting to compare the different names by which the ministry of the Christian Church has come to be known.

If you are an Episcopalian, you will doubtless say that you are being prepared to be a priest in the Church of God. To others, such a claim may seem almost shocking. Some of you belong to denominations which have been so concerned to exalt the priesthood of the laity (a non-biblical expression, not generally used by biblically-minded people) that they have managed to evacuate the work of the ordained ministry of all its priestly significance. If you take that view, you are likely to have a maimed and imperfect view of the meaning of your own work. You cannot have a biblical theology of the ministry, unless you take seriously the doctrine of the Epistle of the Hebrews concerning the heavenly high priesthood of Christ. In accepting the grave responsibility of ordination to the ministry in a Christian body which is itself priestly, you therefore accept also the calling of the Church that you should specially, permanently and responsibly exercise the priestly office. You stand before God on behalf of men, and before men on behalf of God.

Some of you are more likely to say that you are being trained in order that, after ordination, you may be preachers. (Episcopalians are not likely to give that answer. If you have heard much Episcopalian preaching, you might be tempted to an uncharitable guess at the reason why.) In view of the preceding chapter, you will not be tempted to suspect me of taking a low view of the importance of preaching. Nevertheless, I regard it as almost a tragedy in the life of the Protestant communions since the Reformation that they have much too closely identified the work of the ministry with the public preaching of the Word of God. Public preaching is the beginning of the work of the ordained minister, but it is not the end. It is not that preaching is unimportant, but that there is a Scriptural proportion of the faith, which has largely been lost in the Protestant communions, and which must be recovered, if they are to exercise again the fullness of the ministry of the Gospel.

Some of us may prefer to be called ministers. That is a good inoffensive word, on which we can all agree. And the title is in the fullest sense biblical, since it reminds us that we are to be followers of him, who, in the words of the Epistle to the Philippians, "took upon him the form of a servant." The Latin word *minister* means simply servant. The ordained minister is the servant of

the Church, "I am in the midst of you, as he that serv-
eth." St. Paul picks up the thought of the Gospels, and
expresses it once for all in II Corinthians 4:5: "We
preach not ourselves, but Christ Jesus as Lord, and ourselves as your servants for Christ's sake." (Note that he
uses the strongest word of all *as your* servants.) Remember that, if you use this title, you will be in good
company, since *servus servorum Dei*, servant of the
servants of God, is a title of no less a person than the
Pope!

None of these titles has denominational significance,
and any one of us is free to use any of them. But some
of you may find yourselves happier with yet another
designation, that of *pastor*. If so, I cannot but applaud
your choice, since to me too this seems one of the indispensable titles of the ordained servant of God. It takes
us back in thought to Christ, the good shepherd, who
gave his life for the sheep. You may remember that St.
Peter addresses the elders of the churches to which he
writes his first Epistle as shepherds, bidding them "tend
the flock of God which is among you. . . . And when
the chief Shepherd shall be manifested, ye shall receive
the crown of glory that fadeth not away." Christ is the
chief Shepherd; we are to be assistant shepherds under
his orders. Look back to Ezekiel 34, the great Old Testament passage on God as the Shepherd of His people, and
you will obtain many fresh insights into the biblical
meaning of this great and beautiful word.

As we try to understand the *pastoral* relation of the

ordained minister to his flock, we shall find again that in a wonderful way the Apostle Paul is our guide. We so often think of him as a theologian that we are in danger of forgetting that he was also one of the greatest and most articulate of Christian pastors. The Acts of the Apostles depict him as always surrounded by members of the team of younger men, whom he was training and sending out to witness in the places which he was unable to visit himself. The Epistles breathe a most tender and comprehensive pastoral spirit.

Some students become so much concerned with the Epistles to the Romans and the Ephesians that they never get as far as the first Epistle to the Thessalonians. Now it must be admitted that, from the theological standpoint, I Thessalonians is of secondary importance; it is usually reckoned to be one of the earliest, if not the earliest, of the Epistles, and we see Paul trying out his apprentice hand in this style of composition. But from the pastoral point of view, this is perhaps the most important Epistle of all. It is one that the ordained minister should read over and over again, in order to gain fresh inspiration for his work, and in order to test himself, as to how far by Pauline standards he is fulfilling it.

Let us take as the starting point for our meditation to-day a few phrases from the second and third chapters of the Epistle:

We were gentle in the midst of you, as when a nurse cherisheth her own children: even so, being affectionately desirous of you, we were well pleased to impart unto you not the gospel of God only, but also our own souls, because ye were become very dear to us.

Then, a little later, speaking of the pain of separation from them, he says:

But we, brethren, being bereaved of you for a short season, in presence not in heart, endeavored the more exceedingly to see your face with great desire. . . . For what is our hope, or joy, or crown of glorying? Are not even ye, before our Lord Jesus at his coming? For ye are our glory and our joy. . . . For now we live, if ye stand fast in the Lord. . . . The Lord make you to increase and abound in love one toward another, and toward all men, even as we also do toward you; to the end he may establish your hearts unblamable in holiness before our God and Father, at the coming of our Lord Jesus with all his saints. . . . Concerning love of the brethren ye have no need that one write unto you: for ye yourselves are taught of God to love one another.

In another passage, he says, "Ye are in our hearts to die together, and to live together."

In all this, the great authority of the Apostle points us beyond him to another authority greater and higher even than his. In the touching story of the rich young ruler who came to Jesus, we are told that Jesus, looking upon him, loved him. He could discern all the instability and uncertainty of that young man's character; and yet he loved him. In the Gospel of John, we read that Jesus loved Mary and Martha and Lazarus. In the same Gospel, just before that glorious manifestation of what he was, in the washing of the disciples' feet, we read: "Having loved his own which were in the world, he loved them unto the end," or "perfectly."

II

The central mystery of the Gospel is the truth that God loves sinners. Most people do not accept that as truth. They think that, if only people will begin to comb their hair and clean their nails, and become a little respectable, God will begin to love them. But that God loves sinners, just as they are, in their defiance and willfullness, in their squalor, in their loneliness and isolation —that seems too high and incredible to be believed. It is too high and incredible for any rational acceptance. But it is there in the Gospels, not as an abstraction, but in what Jesus was and said and did. And I know that it is true; because in my own pastoral ministry, in the love of the pastor for his flock, I find very faintly and imperfectly the reflection of the love of God, sealed and assured to sinners in the life and death of our Lord.

This love does not depend upon any attractiveness in the sheep. Some of them are by no means attractive with their torn and draggled fleeces, stumbling through the brakes and briers of the wilderness. It does not depend on any virtue in them; if they were virtuous, they would not be sinners in need of redemption. It depends only on the eyes of Christ. If the Spirit of Christ is at work in us at all, we learn to look at men and women, not just as they are, but as through the grace of Christ they can become. The love of the pastor is not sentiment; it is the child of faith and hope—faith in God and hope for man.

That love can be wounded, but it cannot be destroyed. Some of you have been working, as I have, among prisoners. No doubt you have been able to recognize in some of them that the offenses for which they have been most justly sentenced were due to some wayward adventurousness, which by the grace of God can be turned into socially advantageous channels. No doubt, you have been able to assure some of them that, when they come out, they will not be coming into a wholly unwelcoming world; there will be waiting for them at least one friend who believes in them not for what they have been, not even for what they are, but for what through the grace of Christ they can yet become.

Perhaps we are becoming a little too poetical. Let us return to the language of plain prose. If you are to be a successful minister of the Gospel, you must be able just to like folks. It is quite clear that our Lord liked folks. He enjoyed being with ordinary people. He did not go to the house of Mary and Martha and Lazarus in order to fulfill a social duty; he went because he enjoyed being with his friends. I am not sure about the dinner in the house of Simon the Pharisee, where they discourteously failed to bring him water wherewith to wash his feet; that may have been more of a burdensome social obligation, though Jesus made far more of it than that. But in general, he made himself available to people, enjoyed being with them and received with gratitude the gifts of their love.

He liked folks, and so must you. If you do not do it naturally, then you must learn to do it supernaturally. This care for people as individuals is essential to the work of the ministry—so much so that I am sure it is one of the gifts which we can ask of God in faith that it will be given. Some of us are naturally shy. That is a grievous handicap. But we must not lie down under it. It may not be possible for it to be completely cured. But I am sure that there is a great deal that God, in answer to prayer, is able to do about it.

If you like folks, you will find time for them.

Not long ago I was grieved because a young friend of mine left the Church of England and joined the Church of Rome. She gave as one of her reasons that the clergy of the Church of England had not time for people as individuals whereas the Roman Catholic priest had. I know that that is not wholly true; but there is a disturbing element of truth in it, and that for a very plain and inescapable reason. I am quoting from memory, but I believe that there is in the United States one Roman Catholic priest to 650 baptized members of that Church. I cannot quote the parallel figures for the non-Roman churches; but you know as well as I that there are many city churches which are such a network of organizations that there is a constant danger that the minister may find his whole time taken up by serving tables, and have no time left at all for personal ministry to people. I do not know exactly how that danger is to be overcome; I am sure that it must be strenuously resisted. If it ever came about that someone in your church said of you, "Mr. X." or "Father X. is a very good man, but he has no time to attend to people," I am afraid that I should write you off as an effective servant of Jesus Christ.

It is remarkable that so often the greatest and busiest people manage to find time for the individual, and never seem to be in a hurry or out of temper. A friend of mine who is a Methodist told me that during the war he happened to mention to Archbishop Temple that his son was at that time stationed at the Guard's Headquarters in the west end of London. The Archbishop replied that he would try to see something of him. Both father and son thought that this was just formal archiepiscopal politeness. The young man was therefore a little surprised when some time later he received a telephone call from Lambeth Palace asking him to call on the Archbishop at 6:00 P.M. one Saturday. Again, he supposed that he would be given perhaps ten minutes of the Archbishop's time in the middle of a busy evening. Not at all. The Archbishop talked to him for three quarters of an hour, without any appearance of being in a hurry, and then said, "Now I think we had better go to my club and look for some dinner." Altogether he managed to give the best part of two hours to a young man who at that time had no special claim to distinction. I am sure that the Archbishop did not think of himself as doing anything unusual. He enjoyed being with young people and hearing them talk; he felt that he could get to know the mind of the younger generation through spontaneous talk, encouraged by his genius for natural friendliness. And if anyone had said to him, "Your Grace, were you really entertaining a *Methodist?*" his laughter would have shaken the whole house.

I have heard the present Archbishop of Canterbury describe how, on his voyage back from America, he took time off to go all over the ship on which he was traveling, visiting the stokers and the stewards at their work, and in their quarters. At the end of the voyage, the chief steward said to him, "Your Grace, I want you to know that whatever you want to do in the Church, every man on this ship will be behind you. You see, the trouble with most of the clergy is they're too well educated." An opinion which most seminary professors do not share.

If you have that gift of easy, spontaneous friendliness, thank God for it; if not, ask it of God, and claim it as one of the "all things" that shall be added unto us.

III

You are to be a shepherd of the flock. But how do you define your flock?

Here, I think, we shall encounter a difference between the American and the British point of view. It is not primarily the difference between countries which have a state Church, and one which has reduced the separation of Church and State almost to the form of a neurosis. Nor is it primarily a difference between episcopal and

nonepiscopal churches. It is rather the difference between countries which have had a long period of history
in which there was only one Church, and a country in
which from the beginning there was a variety of denominations, even in areas in which in colonial days
there was one established and exclusive Church.

In the early Middle Ages, indeed even before the end
of the Dark Ages, the whole land surface of England was
divided into parishes. In rural parts of England, many of
the parochial boundaries remain exactly as they were at
the time of *Domesday Book*. In every parish was to be
found the parson, *persona ecclesiae*, the official representative of the Church, who was not the minister of a
congregation but the shepherd of a flock, the whole flock
of Christ as it was to be found in the area entrusted to
his care. In course of time, with the growth of divisions
in the Church, that ideal ceased to correspond to the
reality, but it is still the basic principle of ministry in
the Church of England. If people call themselves Roman
Catholics, Methodists or Baptists, it is not the business of
the parson to force himself upon them, but he is there
for them all, and if at any time they wish to call upon
him for his services, they have a perfect right to do so.
He is still *the parson*. I believe that there is hardly a
trace of this parochial system in America, except in some
survivals in the Episcopal Church in Virginia.

You will see at once that, though in practice there may
not be much difference, psychologically the attitude of
a man who takes seriously his responsibility for a whole

area is likely to be very different from that of a man who starts by thinking of the particular group of Christians which comes to worship in his church. To the first, his task presents itself as primarily evangelistic. To the second, evangelism may be only one of those extras for which you have a special committee, and a periodical drive.

It would be impossible, in a country of so many denominations, to attempt to introduce anything like the parochial system. I earnestly hope that you may all have something of the parochial spirit. You are concerned with the nice quiet sheep in the fold. But your first concern must be for the one sheep that has gone astray; except that in so many places, it is the ninety and nine who have gone astray, and only the one tame sheep who is left in the fold.

As a minister, you have been given some sheep, some inside the fold and some outside it. Now that you have got them what do you propose to do with them?

Once again, it is St. Paul who gives us the perfect answer: "Christ in you, the hope of glory: whom we proclaim, admonishing every man and teaching every man in all wisdom that we may present every man perfect in Christ." You will note that the words "every man" occur three times—admonishing every man; that is, awaking him out of the sleep of death and sin; teaching every man, that is, training him in the way of Christian life and devotion; that we may present every man perfect in Christ, the end and fruition of our labor. There is an ideal of pastoral practice for you. Once committed to it, you will never be able to rest until it is fulfilled; and since it never will be fulfilled, you will never be able to rest.

Note that this pastoral ideal makes great demands on faith. First, it calls for faith in the unlimited power of God to restore and renew his creation. Secondly, it calls for great faith in men. That bit of human flotsam that somehow drifts into your sphere is the man whom you are to present perfect in Christ Jesus. It is true that not all will attain to it; but we are not allowed in advance to make distinctions as to those who can become perfect and those who are destined always to remain imperfect.

Some time ago I read a book on pastoral practice written, I regret to say, by two priests of my own Church, in which was set forth the thesis that religious gifts are limited to only a few people, and that of the others who have not this special endowment, the most that can be expected is conformity to the Church's rules, fulfillment of certain duties in regard to church attendance, Christian giving and the like, acceptance of certain rules of personal discipline, and so on. That seems to me one of the most misleading things I have ever read.

It is, of course, true whatever denomination you may happen to belong to, that the majority of your good churchgoers will be living under law and not under grace. The heart of man is incurably legalistic; and that is the form, or rather the deformation, of the Christian faith in which men find it easiest to accept it. They prefer the limited demands of an ecclesiastical system, heavy though they may be, to the unlimited demands of genuine surrender to Jesus Christ. Within its own limits, legalism may produce admirable types of character. The Pharisees were by no means contemptible people; they had a zeal for the law of God, and a devotion to it that would put many Christians to shame. The trouble is that what law can achieve is always limited, since the most that it can effect is modification of character from without, and not transformation from within. That inner transformation can really begin only when a man passes from the sphere of law to that of grace, from the status of a servant to that of a son.

The danger for us, as ministers of the Gospel, is that we may fall into the error of this double classification, and accept the idea that the best of which most people are capable is to lead a reasonably decent life under the law. It is much easier to produce good church members than to produce Christians. I must confess to feeling deeply anxious whenever I hear anyone described as a good churchman; I have the feeling, perhaps wrongly, that that means that he is not a very good Christian, that he has stopped short with the fulfillment of the outward and comparatively easy duties, and has never entered at all into the peril and the passion of a real encounter with Jesus Christ.

The trouble about the law is that it tends to produce the dullness of uniformity; it is the glory of the Gospel that it enhances the distinctiveness that makes a man really himself and not someone else.

Everything in the modern world tends to conformity. Mass production has influenced what we read and what we hear and what we wear to such an extent that the threat to personal existence is a serious menace throughout the Western world. The totalitarian regimes have their own special methods of checking dangerous thoughts and producing a drab sameness among all the millions of their people. But do not imagine that this is a special evil of the twentieth century. In all primitive societies, the regimentation of life is carried further than would be endured in the most conventional small town in the Middle West; every act of life is ruled and determined by custom, and woe betide the individualist who attempts at one single point to go outside the limits of the established tradition.

Some modern writers draw a distinction between the *individual* and the *person*. I am not sure whether the distinction is a valid one, but it is certainly convenient. The individual is the man who is afraid of his separateness from his fellows. The person is the man who has begun to develop from within himself his infinite capacity for being different from other men, and therefore for making an authentic contribution of his own to the life of his community, his nation or his church. Perhaps Kierkegaard was right, when he said that man becomes real only in the lonely and awful experience of meeting with Christ. I sometimes wonder whether the doctrine of the

Holy Spirit is not the right starting point for the doctrine of personality in man, and whether any man can rightly be called a person, until that spirit in him, which the book of Proverbs calls the candle of the Lord, has been kindled by direct contact with God revealed in the face of Jesus Christ. My experience of the astonishing change wrought by genuine conversion among poor and ignorant village people in India leads me to think that there may be something to be said for this view.

If we can rightly apply this idea to our work of ministry, you can see at once what a difference it would make to our expectation of Christian response. Under law, the response of good church membership is monotonously similar. Inevitably law reduces things to a common denominator. The conscientious performance of the same actions produces in time the same type of character. Under grace, everything is completely different. Individual difference is encouraged; even if it were not encouraged it would assert itself. Each Christian becomes an authentic witness, since each has his own experience of Christ, incommensurable with that of any other person, since all genuinely personal experiences are individual and unique. Each is able to make his own irreplaceable contribution to the life of the whole. Each has his own instrument to play, his own gift to offer to the harmony of the whole orchestra. It may be, by comparison with some others, a rather insignificant instrument; its note may be low and indistinctly heard among so many; but the Conductor, who knows the whole score, is looking for that particular note and expecting it, and will miss it if it is not there.

Someone may object that if we encourage the individual to exercise his Christian liberty, the result may be a wild individualism, in which fellowship and the sense of responsibility will be lost. I reply at once that in the life of the Church, the two elements of liberty and discipline must always be held together. But it is only in the light of liberty that discipline becomes significant. The possession of an instrument, and some capacity to blow, does not immediately qualify a performer for a place in a great symphony orchestra; he must learn to follow every beat of the conductor's hand, to adapt himself to others, to understand his contribution in relation to the whole; only then will his performance be acceptable. But without the trained capacity of individuals, each with his different instrument, there could be no rendering of the symphony at all.

 I am still on the point that you must not set any limits to your expectation of what the Holy Spirit can do for and through the people whom you are called to serve. On one occasion Moses is recorded to have said, "Would that all the Lord's people were prophets," with the fairly clear understanding that it was most unlikely that they ever would be. But we are to utter the same prayer with the expectation that it will be fulfilled. Moses spoke under the old dispensation, when seventy men were chosen out as the representatives of the people; we speak under the new dispensation of which the sign is that the Spirit is to be poured out upon all flesh.

This is the second point at which the true democracy of the Christian faith is manifest. We are all one in our starting point as sinners. We are all one in our vocation to be saints. Of course, there are diversities of function in the one body, as there are diversities of instruments in an orchestra. I probably take a higher view of the ministry, with its special functions and authority, than many of you would take. I think that there is a distinct contribution to be made by the woman, which is different from that which can be made by the man; the weakness of the so-called feminist movement of the earlier years of this century was that it was so largely a masculinist movement, an attempt to show that women can do as well as men all the things which men can do well. But underneath these diversities there is the essential oneness of vocation—that we are all called to be saints.

IV

If you take this view of your people and of your ministry among them, you will condemn yourself to a life of perpetual dissatisfaction, because the goal always recedes as you advance toward it. We can set no limits to what the Holy Spirit can achieve in the reshaping of this refractory material of human personality. Yet a divine dissatisfaction remains. It bears no relation to the restlessness of the minister who is always wanting to move on or to get on. It is simply the recognition that both we and our people are imperfect, and that what God wants to do for us and through us is always being hindered by the weakness of our faith and the faintness of our zeal. Such dissatisfaction is a permanent safeguard against complacency in the exercise of the ministry.

If this dissatisfaction is part of your experience, you will find that it constantly drives you to your knees, in prayer for yourself and for your flock. No part of the work to which we are called is more important than the ministry of intercession, the hidden task of praying ceaselessly for the flock and for the members of the flock. Intercession is perhaps the easiest part of prayer— not that any part of prayer is really easy. It is the kind of prayer in which we may most readily hope to see the answers to our prayers. It is not so difficult to pray for those whom we love; and the immediate reward of our intercession is that through it we come to love them more. And yet, strangely enough, serious and detailed intercession is little practiced even by ministers of the Gospel.

In every aspect of our relationship to God, we touch upon mystery. We cannot tell how intercessory prayer works; we do not know how God takes our prayers, and uses them to bring blessing to those for whom we pray. But we do a great many things everyday, even in ordinary life, without full understanding of all the processes involved. Some of us are quite content to press the self-starter of a car without trying to understand the mystery of why something happens when we do. I have long felt that the last word on the subject was really said by Archbishop Temple when, with his massive common sense, he remarked, "I notice that, if I am praying for my friends, coincidences happen; if I stop praying for my friends, the coincidences stop." That is precisely my own experience. Answers to prayer are evidential only to the one who has prayed and to no one else; if you tell others about the answers to your prayers, you will bore them as much as if you tell them your dreams. But I do not believe that any Christian can pray steadily and regularly for specific, limited objects, particularly if those objects are people, without receiving the assurance that mysterious forces are being let loose in the spiritual world, and that something is really being achieved.

Almost all the great leaders I have known in the Church have been great men of prayer.

One of my most intimate friends in the Indian Church was our first great Indian bishop, Vedanayagiam Samuel Azariah. He came originally from the area in which I was working, though his own great work was done six hundred miles to the north among the Telugus. We sat together for years on the committee that was producing the new Tamil version of the Bible. One day he remarked quite casually that he found time to pray everyday by name for everyone in a position of leadership in his diocese. I suppose that meant about thirty people, apart from those who were remembered less frequently. You will not be surprised to learn that he rose every day at 4:30 A.M. in order to find time for his prayers. (In South India, you are not taken seriously as a Christion unless you are out of bed by 5:00 A.M. at the latest. Intending missionaries, please note!) Nor will you be surprised to learn that, with such leadership at the top, the number of Christians increased threefold during Azariah's episcopate of thirty years, and that the Church developed steadily in self-support, in evangelistic zeal and in capacity for responsible self-government.

Tell me whom you pray for, and I will tell you the quality of your spiritual life.

I was talking not long ago to a younger friend who has recently become a schoolmaster, with, I think, a real sense of Christian vocation. I asked him if he prayed for his boys. He said, "Yes, when they get into trouble." I thought it might be rather a good idea to pray for them before they got into trouble, and told him so. Another younger friend said in conversation, "I have no one specially to pray for in Geneva." I suggested that he might try praying for me; he looked a little astonished, and said, "Do bishops need to be prayed for? Do you know, I had never thought of that!" Alas, poor bishops!

A serious ministry of intercession demands time, self-discipline and a certain amount of system.

You will not pray for people regularly unless you write down their names. You cannot pray for everyone; there must be an element of selection. Before you add any name to your prayer list, you should consider seriously whether that person is one whom God seems definitely to have put within your field of spiritual responsibility. Any prayer list should be revised every three months; especially as an ordained minister, you will find that some whose names have been on your list have moved out of your area of responsibility, and can rightly be left to the care of others.

People vary so much in their capacity for prayer and in the methods that they find useful that I do not think it would be useful to go further into detail. I will only add three detached remarks. From my own experience I have long since concluded that the only way to arrange a prayer list is alphabetically; any other system of classification becomes in time maddeningly complicated. If you make a start, and follow the practice of praying for people once a week, you will find that the number of those for whom you can pray with feeling and understanding is far greater than you had imagined possible. If you persevere, you will find that the desire for this kind of ministry grows upon you, and that increasingly it can be carried out not only in set times of prayer, but in those odd moments throughout the day, when the mind is otherwise unoccupied and thought is free.

V

Let me add only one more touch to the picture I am trying to draw today. If you are to be a faithful minister of Christ, as soon as possible you must set your people to work for Christ.

It is not always those who talk most about the priesthood of the laity who are the most willing to let the lay folk exercise their priestly ministry. Remember that the priesthood of the unordained member of the Church is not fulfilled by sitting on the church board and managing the church finance. That is admirable necessary service. But it constitutes those who perform it not priests but Levites; and I fear that some of you are destined in time to come to suffer from the Levitical spirit of your leading laymen.

There is a tendency for the ordained minister to wish to create a minister's church. His position must always be central. It is he who appears in the pulpit Sunday by Sunday. Much of the direction and much of the spiritual initiative must rest in his hands. It is easy to go beyond this, and to concentrate all spiritual authority and all spiritual leadership in the hands of the minister, leaving to the layman only the external and administrative tasks. This is not the Church, as the New Testament understands the term.

We have said over and over again that the minister has a special function within the Church, for which he is solemnly set apart, and which gives him a representative and priestly function within the priestly body. It is our good friend and guide St. Paul who, once again, defines for us exactly what that function is; it is to train the faithful in order that they may be ministers of God. In the great passage on the Church in Ephesians 4 we read: "He gave some to be apostles; and some prophets; and some, evangelists; and some pastors and teachers; for the perfecting of the saints unto the work of ministering, unto the building up of the body of Christ." In many English versions, and in some Greek texts, you will find a comma between *saints* and *unto;* but in, for example, Nestle's Greek text, there is no comma, and I am sure that this is right. All these special gifts are given in the Church, with a view to training the saints, that is, the ordinary members, who have received no such special gifts, in order that they may be ministers, and may themselves contribute directly to the building up of the body of Christ.

In the churches of the continent of Europe, the word *diakonia*, here translated *ministry*, tends to be limited to such ministries of the Church as philanthropic and humanitarian service. A member of one of those churches reading this passage might think that it was only for such "lay" services as these that the ordinary members of the Church were to be trained. I can only refer you to a concordance. You will find that *diakonia* is used in the widest frame of reference, including the specifically spiritual as well as the more secular ministries. For these also our lay folk are to be trained.

Is it possible?

Your answer to that question will depend on your answer to the prior question as to what we are to expect of God in relation to our people, and of our people in relation to God. Do you believe that it is possible for your ordinary layman to have a personal experience of the grace of God in Jesus Christ, to receive the gift of the

Holy Spirit, and to bear his own individual witness to what he has seen and heard? If not, of course, there is no more to be said; you will have a pleasant life training up generations of robots. If you do, then all we have to ask is how that individual gift is to be developed, and how it is to be used, not individualistically, but in relation to the life of the Body of Christ.

If we could get our lay folk working as spirit-filled ministers of the Gospel, how many of our problems would be solved.

We are all faced by the perplexity of the inaccessibility of modern life to the Gospel. In the simple social structure of earlier days, the minister could go everywhere, meet everyone, and play his part in determining the conditions under which men lived. Now he cannot. Industrial chaplaincies have their use. But, in point of fact, if the Gospel is to be proclaimed in the factory and the dock, on ships at sea, in legislatures and penitentiaries, it can be done only by Christian laymen, who make the place of their professional occupation also the place of their Christian witness. As some of you know from experience, that is in general a harder task than that which is faced by the ordained minister in his parish.

I have been encouraged by what I have read of the method of visitation evangelism in this country. Some ministers have found the right way of using this method. They have carefully trained groups of laymen over a period, and then sent them out two and two to visit, not merely to invite people to come to Church, but to bear clear testimony to what Christ has done for them. This simple proclamation by lay-people seems to be wonderfully effective. When you or I preach, there is always a suspicion in the minds of some people that we do it just because we have to—it is the job for which we are paid. When busy lay folk, especially men, are prepared to go out two evenings a week in all weather, and to undertake the extremely trying work of knocking at the doors of perfect strangers, even those who have not the least desire to accept the message realize that there must be something in it.

But, if our people are to do this kind of work, they must be trained for it. And that is where the ordained minister comes in.

They must be taught the Word of God, experimentally, but with a sufficient theological basis to enable them to answer the questions that modern man is likely to ask.

They must be taught to pray. It cannot be assumed that they will know how to pray, unless they are given some guidance by those who have gone a little further in the life of prayer.

They do not need to be taught "evangelistic techniques"—what horrible jargon we produce in our technocratic age—but they must be given some help in recognizing pitfalls by the way and in avoiding them. They must be bold enough not to be afraid of making mistakes in the service of the Lord, and humble enough to learn by their mistakes.

Above all they must be taught to expect that something will happen as a result of their work. Some schools of theology at the present time insist that the task of the Church is just to bear witness to what God has done, and to leave results entirely to him. This is a half-truth, and like all half-truths dangerous. We must do justice also to the meaning of St. Paul when he says, "I am become all things to all men, *that I may by all means save some.*" We might hesitate to use his language; we have no right to deny the relevance of his thought for today. The great Baptist preacher Charles Haddon Spurgeon once asked his students: "Do you expect to see conversions every time you preach?"; and when the students with becoming modesty replied, "Well, no; not *every* time," Spurgeon's rather unkind comment was, "And of course that's why you don't see them." Like many great preachers, Spurgeon was oversimplifying the matter. But was he not much nearer being right than those who seem to take it for granted that nothing will ever happen in the Church, and who would be almost distressed if the Word of God on their lips ever showed signs of being effective in the thing to which he had sent it?

The attitude of the minister must always be that of John the Baptist: "He must increase, but I must decrease."

Of course, this is true in relation to the Master. If you are setting yourself up, Christ cannot be glorified; Christ can be glorified only if you are willing to be hidden.

But in a real sense the same applies in the relation between the minister and his people. We can almost say that the less the minister does in a parish, the better organized that parish will be. Of course, as far as possible, you will leave all financial and purely administrative work to the laymen; not because such work is in any way to be despised, but because you were not ordained to serve tables, but to give yourself to the ministry of the word and to prayer. But also you will do well to leave as much as you can of the aggressive and more directly spiritual work to the lay folk. Your special task is to concentrate on deep knowledge of the Scriptures, on understanding the faith, on steady teaching, on personal pastoral care, and on the ministry of intercession.

Train your lay folk, and send them out to do the jobs. If they get the credit for what is going on, rejoice in that too. Be content yourself to be the quiet, unobtrusive influence, through whom new life comes into the parish. Let them be seen, let them be exalted, let Christ be glorified in them. Then you may sit back and feel that you are beginning to do the work for which you were ordained

⚔ 5 ⚔

The Minister and the World

I

"Again the devil taketh him unto an exceeding high mountain, and sheweth him all the kingdoms of the world, and the glory of them; And he saith unto him, All these things will I give thee, if thou wilt fall down and worship me."

It has often been noticed that the severest temptations may come to us through things which are not evil in themselves. If we are seriously trying to follow Christ, that which is blatantly evil is likely to repel us; the insidious and dangerous allurements are those which can present themselves in the form of good.

In actual fact, a great deal of what we have been taught to regard as sin can be classified as willful error of time, place or measure, in relation to that which in its own time and place and in its proper measure is good. Unless we fall into the Manichaean error, which would condemn all pleasure as suspect, if not positively evil in itself, we shall recognize that God himself has appointed pleasant things as part of our portion in life. The right use of them is blessed; it is only the impatience which snatches at them, before the time has come, or the ill-controlled judgment which values them more highly than is their due, or the self-indulgence which refuses to surrender them, that can turn what in itself is good into the source of great evil. The fault of the prodigal son was that he snatched untimely at an inheritance which was his own, and which would have come to him, had he not unseasonably demanded it, at the time appointed by the father. Even in the realm of sex, that thorny perplexity of the human race, is it not clear that most of the evil things men do result from wilful error in relation to time, in snatching at this good gift of God, before the appointed time has come; or of place, in going outside the narrow limits that he has appointed for the welfare of the individual and of society or of measure, in excessive self-indulgence, where the law of God commands restraint and self-control?

In the third temptation of our Lord, we recognize this factor of possible evil coming in under the disguise of acknowledged good. He knew that he had been appointed by the Father to lordship over all the world. What the devil was offering was merely the inheritance which was already his own. But there are right ways and wrong ways of entering into an inheritance. Under the symbolic form of the narrative, which must have come to us from the Lord himself, since he alone can have communicated to the disciples what had passed in that lonely period of testing, Christian interpretation has discerned his wrestling with the problem of the methods that he was to employ in seeking and establishing a kingdom.

The expectation of the Jews looked for a Messiah, who would appear in warlike power, and overthrow the usurped dominion of the Romans. The pious Jew could point to many passages in the Old Testament, in which the coming of the Kingdom of God was set forth in the imagery of war and of destruction. To Jesus also, these ancient sayings were Holy Scripture. It was necessary that he should ponder them, and make up his mind as to their bearing on the nature of the warfare that he was to wage. We underestimate the reality of his humanity if we take it for granted that the answer was immediately obvious, that there was no temptation, and that the instruments of worldly success could be at once dismissed as having no place in the mission which God had committed to his hands.

Whatever else men may think about Jesus of Nazareth, they are constrained to admit that he was superbly endowed with the gifts of leadership, and with capacity to bind men and women to himself in deathless loyalty. In his contemporaries and fellow countrymen, he had better material to work upon than we are sometimes given to suppose. Some years ago, when a Jewish undergraduate said to me, "If it comes to fighting in Palestine, the young men of the Haganah will just eat up the Arabs," I was inclined to discount his words as the expression of a slightly pathetic national loyalty. But after all he was right. The Arabs have imposed upon the world the picture of themselves as a great fighting race. Our emotional picture of the Jew (I speak perhaps rather for Britain than for America) is too much based on recollections of Shylock—"for sufferance is the badge of all our tribe"—and of Fagin in *Oliver Twist*. We forget that in the time of Christ, the Jews were known as a surly and stubborn race, good fighters and implacable enemies. Forty years after his death, the Jews, divided and ill-led as they were, held out for years with fanatical courage against the whole might of Rome, and gave to the self-confidence of the Empire the worst shock that it endured until the menace from the northern barbarians became overwhelming. What could not Jesus have made of them, if, coming to them as an earthly leader, he had brought to their cause his calm wisdom, his knowledge of the human heart, and his power to lift men above the best that they knew of themselves?

The temptation was faced and overcome. It is not clear from the record whether Jesus himself knew exactly what he was doing when he rejected the way of force; in the light of later events, we can see quite clearly that he was in fact signing his own death warrant; from that moment the shadow of the Cross begins to fall upon his path.

II

The servant is not greater than his Lord. From time to time the devil has led the Church of Christ up to the same high mountain and confronted it with the same temptation. It is the will of God that all the kingdoms of the world should become the kingdom of our God and of his Christ. But how is that purpose of the ages to be accomplished? Again and again the Church has succumbed to the temptation of thinking that the way marked out by Christ is too slow and too costly, has convinced itself that divine purposes can be worked out by human means, and has cheerfully taken to itself the whole armor of man.

In A.D. 313, Constantine, lifting the Church from the depths of persecution to the heights of imperial favor, made Christianity the religion of the state. With horrifying rapidity, the Church accepted the idea that the arm of the state might be called in to help in the establishment of the truth. I have long regarded the year A.D. 383 as one of the most disastrous turning points in history, since in that year for the first time, in the condemnation of the Spanish heretic Priscillian, the blood of Christians was shed by Christians.

In the Middle Ages and after, the identification of the spiritual power with the temporal was so close, and the control exercised by the Church over the minds and conscience of men was so exact and rigid, that it was almost impossible for that Church to escape from the corruption that seems almost always to accompany the exercise of power. In the sixteenth century, we find Francis Xavier, purest and most devoted of Roman Catholic missionaries, writing to the king of Portugal to urge that the Inquisition should be introduced into India, as an indispensable aid to the work of evangelization, and unfortunately securing a favorable answer to his request.

We do ill to cast stones at our predecessors in an earlier age. In the nineteenth century, the same temptation befell the Western churches in a different form. Missionaries from the West went out to every corner of the world, carrying with them the Gospel, but carrying also a great deal of Western arrogance and self-confidence which had very little to do with the principles of Jesus Christ. There was a tendency to think that wherever Western arms, Western commerce, Western civilization penetrated, they would of themselves bring some kind of deliverance to the nations, and help to prepare the way for the coming of the kingdom of Christ. Those who lived under this illusion had better reason for their dreams than is always admitted today. Our Western civilization, for all its gigantic defects, has been deeply penetrated by the Gospel of Christ. Imperfectly, it has tried to live by certain convictions as to human worth and integrity, which have not been characteristic of any other great civilization. Nevertheless, the illusion was illusion. The kingdom of Christ can come by the methods of Christ in no other way. It is possible both to recognize the unexampled splendor of the missionary enterprise of the nineteenth century, and to be aware of the naïveté of some of the hopes entertained by Christians in that period, and the confusion of thought that under-

lay some expectations of a speedy triumph of the Gospel
in the world.

III

Today the ever-oscillating pendulum of Christian
thought has swung almost to the other extreme. The
Church has become so acutely aware of the temptations
latent in all thought of world-wide dominion that it is
almost unwilling to make the pilgrimage to the mountaintop, and to let either God or devil show it the glory
of the kingdoms that have been redeemed by Christ. The
failure of nerve which is so widespread in the West in
our day has worked also as a solvent of Christian hope
and enterprise.

In the middle of the nineteenth century, it was assumed that "we are all Christians now." With bland
short-sightedness, it was taken for granted that Christian
ethics would survive the abandonment of Christian doctrine, and that the West was permanently committed to
"Christian civilization." At that time, Kierkegaard was
almost alone in his protest against the whole idea of
"Christendom." To him, Christ was always a contemporary challenge and offense; nineteen centuries of
Christian history could afford no guarantee whatsoever
that the men of today would react better to that offense
than the contemporaries of Jesus Christ who crucified
him. Subsequent events have read a grim significance
into words that when written seemed to spring from an
irrelevant and unjustified pessimism.

In our century, the bluff of Christendom has been called.

"Holy Russia" has become the center and archpropagator of a system which has accepted as one of its primary aims the destruction of Christianity as of every other religious faith. The Russian Church has survived the terrible days of persecution; but it seems to some sympathetic observers that it has purchased a shorter spoon than is altogether handy for those who must needs sup with the devil. After Hitler's advent to power in 1933, the resistance of the Confessing Church has added glorious pages to Christian history; but the record of those days shows that the majority of Christians in Germany were unable to discern the signs of the times, and were willing to accord their loyalty to a system which, whatever its real origin, owed nothing to Nazareth or Galilee.

Today, the old antithesis between the Christian West and the non-Christian East has almost ceased to have any meaning for us. We are so burdened with the sense of the weaknesses and injustices of our societies that we wonder whether it is legitimate in any sense to talk of a Christian civilization.

We must not suppose that we are the first generation to have a lively sense of those imperfections and injustices. No writer of today has denounced social evils more pungently than Ruskin and Carlyle. But there is a real difference in attitude. In these more buoyant days it was assumed that evils had only to be denounced, and that then action would be taken to cure them; it was believed that there was in Christian society an immense fund of intelligence and good will, which could be mobilized and directed toward infinitely extensible goals of human progress. Our more jaded age seems to feel that the fault is not in the superstructure but in the foundations, and to question whether there is anything that can really be done about it, except to talk pathetically about the guilt of the Church and its need for penitence.

The old civilizations of Europe have been hardest hit by this change of climate. For a number of years, Europe has been told very firmly both by Russia and by America that it is finished and has no future. When those two great world powers, which disagree on everything else, agree on this one point, it is difficult for Europe not to believe that there may be something in it. In France and Germany nihilism and despair have taken so deep a hold on the minds of the young as gravely to menace their power of recovery. In Britain, except for some professionally pessimistic circles, the situation is not so bad. In that still-favored land, the vigor and variety of intellectual life, technological inventiveness, and an incomparable versatility and nimbleness in political adjustment give the lie to any idea of serious racial exhaustion or degeneracy. But Britain too is exposed to the ceaseless barrage of menacing prophecy from both East and West. Why America, to which the survival of Western Europe is so indispensably necessary, should work so hard for the deterioration of one of its own most precious assets is one of those mysteries which the European mind will never be able to penetrate.

But America itself has not escaped unscathed by the acids of the modern world. Nothing is more surprising to the European visitor than the failure of American nerve in face of the new problems of world leadership. For this your own prophets have been in part responsible. Nowhere in the world have denunciations of the selfishness and corruption of Western society and of its insoluble inner contradictions been more severe than here. Confronted with the undoubted fact of the increase of church membership in almost all denominations in the United States, the critic tends to inveigh against this as no more than the search for respectability of a still-rising middle class, and as further evidence of the alliance between the Western churches and the *bourgeoisie*. Point out to him the solid virtues of that churchgoing middle class, and he may reply that this is simply the continuation west of the Atlantic of the gigantic Victorian hypocrisy, from which Europe is now happily being delivered.

When all this rains upon us from so many respectable quarters, it is not surprising that sometimes we are left in doubt as to the nature of our Christian vocation. If our so-called Christian civilization is really as bad as it is painted, have we anything to offer to the non-Christian nations of Africa and the East? If we are entangled ourselves in an evil system, can we open our mouths in courageous Christian witness? Has the Church any right to go up to the top of the mount to stand with Christ, or with the devil, in contemplation of the kingdoms of the world?

Our visitors from the "younger churches" have not done much to restore our self-confidence. They have told us ceaselessly of the harm wrought in their countries by Western aggression, whether political, as in the case of Britain, or economic, as in the case of America. They have suggested that missionaries, perhaps unknown to themselves, have been actuated by imperialistic motives, and have served not so much as ambassadors of Christ as instruments of the obscure political purposes of Western powers. Some assert roundly that from the beginning missionaries have done more harm than good.

IV

Where are we then, standing between our conviction of the lordship of Christ and his claims on us, and the situation of our contemporary world?

Some of our prophets tell us that there is no course open to the Church other than that of returning to the catacombs. For centuries the Church has lived in and on the Constantinian situation of alliance with the state and dependence on it. That situation has now come to an end. War has been declared again between Christ and the powers of the world. It is only prudence to recognize that fact, to prepare ourselves to go underground, and to make the survival of the Church until better times our primary concern.

Others, not prepared to go so far as this, tell us that the one duty laid upon the Church today is repentance—repentance for past arrogance and blindness and betrayal of the cause of Christ. To some extent I am in agreement. The Church can never represent more than very imperfectly the kingdom of God upon earth, and, therefore, penitence is the permanent condition of its life. I am bound to protest against any suggestion that penitence can be a substitute for action. In the New Testament I find that penitence is always regarded as a stimulus to action, and as a precondition for it.

Now since there is in all of us a strong tendency to take the line of least resistance, and to rationalize our weaknesses into virtues, we may easily confuse ourselves into mistaking refusal of the will of God for obedience to it. Was not Judah condemned for refusing the waters of Siloah that go softly, and desiring the waters of the river great and strong? May it not be that, at this point in the history of the Church, it would be arrogance to go up to the top of the mountain and look out on the kingdoms of the world? Shall we not do better to stay in the quiet valley, by the streams that flow softly, content to cultivate our garden, without desiring the land of wide distances and far horizons? Is not the God of the mountaintop the God also of the valleys? Has not he created also the waters of Siloah?

For us in the Episcopal Church, and perhaps espe-

cially in England, the waters of Siloah do go so very
softly. You are familiar with the picture of the gray old
village church, amid its tall trees, in an atmosphere of
peace, where nothing seems to have changed since the
beginning of the world. My last English home was like
that, my father's last parish before his retirement. The
beautiful fourteenth century church was just across the
garden from the rectory; beyond it was one of the most
beautiful villages in England, bowered amid immemorial
trees. Of course, even in that garden there were disap-
pointments and frustrations; and yet it was a place of
peace and tranquil beauty.

Do not suppose for a moment I underestimate the importance of the quiet rural ministry. It is a necessary
part of the ministry of the Church. I have often pointed
out that many of the books that have made Christian
history have been written in country rectories—Richard
Hooker's *The Laws of Ecclesiastical Polity*, William
Law's *Serious Call to a Devout and Holy Life*, George
Herbert's *Temple* and *A Priest to the Temple*, John
Keble's *Christian Year*, and a dozen others. But we must
not mistake the part for the whole; we must not mistake
a temporary crisis for a permanent or long-lasting situation. The Church is sometimes called to a period of quiet
and recollection, but only that it may recover its strength
for advance. The call to the Church, and particularly to
the candidate for the ministry, as he looks out on his
lifework, is always to go up to the top of the mount and
to survey the kingdoms of the world, which are pre-

destined to become the kingdoms of our God and of his Christ.

V

It is rather fashionable at the present time to affirm that Christ has already been constituted by God the Father as Lord of all the world, and that the task of the Church is simply to proclaim an already existing lordship of Christ. Theologically I am in full agreement; every time I say in the Creed, "He ascended into heaven and sitteth at the right hand of God the Father Almighty," that is exactly what I am affirming. And yet I want that theological affirmation to be translated in terms of present reality. What does the lordship of Christ mean, for instance, in Tibet, where there is no Church and no proclamation of the world of God at all? How does the reality of the lordship of Christ help men, who have never even so much as heard his name—and that means at least a third of the men and women now living in the world? The lordship of Christ is a fact. Yet is it not also true that that lordship is everywhere unknown or resisted or ignored or denied?

The statement that it is the task of the Church to proclaim the lordship of Christ is meaningless, unless it is understood in the sense that it is the business of the Church, through the power of the Holy Spirit, to see that the lordship of Christ is made effective throughout the whole world, in every realm and area of man's life, and in the experience of every single individual born into the world. Nothing less than this is involved in the command of Christ to his people to be witnesses in Judaea and in Jerusalem and in Samaria and unto the ends of the earth.

In our survey of the kingdoms of the world, we may pick out three areas in which in particular the lordship of Christ is today being denied and ignored, and in which, therefore, the Church is called to mobilize and concentrate its forces for advance.

VI

First, there is the general intellectual climate of the age. This climate is made up of a very large number of hardly discernible forces—the books and papers that men read, the significance that words have come to have for them, the standards of value by which their judgments and their actions are determined. No analysis of these hidden processes of thought and reaction can ever be finally exhaustive. Yet it is clear that the climate of some periods is favorable to the Christian faith, whereas that of others is unfavorable, and that we live at what is perhaps the peak of one of those periods in which faith is difficult.

The writers of fiction of an age may serve as a convenient, though not wholly accurate, gauge of the intellectual and moral standards of those who read their works. It is plain that almost all the great English novelists of the Victorian Age, even those who, like George Eliot, were very far from being orthodox Christians, had been profoundly influenced by the traditions and standards of the Christian Gospel and the Christian ethic. Even when they wrote about the evil that is in the world, and they did so with a frankness that would surprise those who have been brought up on the mythology of Victorian prudery, they wrote with sternness and pity, as against the background of what they believed to be the unchanging laws of a moral universe. That is to say, they were fully aware of evil, but they were not immersed in it. Today, that is no longer so. The subjects dealt with by modern writers are not so very different from those of their predecessors, but the stable moral background has almost wholly disappeared. Personally I find that a course of reading in contemporary fiction is a desolating experience. So many modern writers seem to imagine that they can write solely about uninteresting and unattractive people, and yet perform the miracle of writing interesting and attractive books. They do not seem to me to have brought off any miracles. Not long ago, I sat down and read straight through one of the best known of modern novels by one of the most highly commended of contemporary authors; the story was sordid and painful, without any of the splendor of tragedy; in the whole book, I could not find one single normally decent or likeable person.

The trouble, of course, is that even Christians are far more affected by this contemporary climate than they realize. Our Christian faith ought to be the determining factor in our whole intellectual and emotional life, a regulating principle which permeates every part of the conscious mind, and makes its way deep into those subconscious levels where spontaneous reactions are so largely determined. Many of us suffer from a painful dichotomy. Most of our conscious thoughts and more of our subconscious attitudes are determined by the contemporary climate of opinion, and our Christian faith remains a separate and unassimilable block in a world to which it does not belong.

Modern education does not greatly help us. At the beginning of the century, the unnecessary but bitter conflict between science and religion held the field. Today, science has learned to be a little more modest in its claims, and the theologians appreciate better than they did the significance of scientific method and the scientific outlook on the world. Now the trouble comes from a different quarter. My experience of American and Canadian universities suggests to me that in many places the faculties of philosophy, psychology, sociology, and sometimes of history as well, are presenting a view of the world in which no place is left for religion, or indeed for any absolute at all; in some places, these disciplines seem not merely to exclude the Christian Gospel, but to present an alternative gospel of their own. And these, after all, are the faculties in which the largest number of students is to be found.

For a change in the general intellectual climate of an age, we must look not so much to the preacher as to the imaginative writer, since it is only through the touching of the imagination that intellectual conviction acquires driving force. There are signs today of the emergence of a new race of Christian imaginative writers. Mr. T. S. Eliot and Mr. Christopher Fry, significant in themselves, may be yet more significant as the forerunners of a new age. I have sometimes wondered how much the crowds which filled the theaters really understood of the subtle dialectic of *The Cocktail Party*. The fact that the theaters were crowded does seem to indicate that folk are beginning to realize again the place of the spiritual in life, and that Mr. Eliot has found the means to convey to them more than they can perhaps grasp by processes of strictly intellectual understanding.

I must not develop this theme at greater length. Few of you will be called to be imaginative writers. Some of you may have a subsidiary role to play as imaginative preachers. All of you should take the trouble to be aware of contemporary currents in thought, and to qualify yourselves, as far as possible, to be mediators between your people and the best that is coming to birth in the world about them.

VII

The second field in which the lordship of Christ has to be asserted anew, or for the first time, is the world of man in "modern mass society." It is clear that in most parts of the world, the Church has lost its contact with the working class in industry. This is perhaps less true in America and Canada than elsewhere; yet even here the phenomenon is on its way, and the churches have not yet taken sufficiently serious cognizance of it.

Just why this separation between the Church and the working man has taken place over such wide areas it is a little difficult to say.

In part it is due to the hard demographic fact of the enormous growth of populations since the beginning of the nineteenth century, in part to the shift of populations, and to the crowding of vast masses of human beings into the tentacular cities of modern times. I have not seen accurate figures of the population of the great cities of the world at different periods; but I think that the number of cities with more than a million inhabitants has trebled itself already in this century. In the countries of Europe, where the churches had inherited the traditional organization of the Middle Ages, it has been found very hard to make the system flexible enough to meet contemporary needs. The more adaptable Free Churches have done noble work, but still far short of what needs to be done. The number of ordained ministers has not kept pace with the rapid growth of populations.

The development of modern industry has led to a rigidity of class distinctions formerly unknown. The Marxist doctrine of the class struggle has had something to do with this, but does not wholly account for it. No one would wish to go back to the old feudal system with its inequalities and injustices; yet that was a system in which men of different ranks of life were bound to-

gether by a sense of mutual responsibilities and obligations, just as the members of different castes in India
today are bound together across the injustices and inequalities of that system, by many threads of common
and mutual loyalties. Today a rapidly increasing part of
the world's population belongs to an industrial proletariat, which is intensely conscious of its own unity, and
of its alienation from everything outside itself. Society is
coming to consist not of classes bound together by mutual loyalties, but of groups the only link between which
are mutual antipathies and mutual dreads.

One acute observer in France, where the situation is
perhaps more strained than elsewhere, has described it in
the following terms: this "is always the class that is not
a class, the class that is beyond society, the class of the
outsiders, the class whose self-assertion can only imply
the subversion of society as it stands . . . that profound
distrust which the working world has for everything
outside itself, and the ruling classes' dread of it . . .
whether such dread seek to disarm the working-class by
concessions or break it by coercion."

This class tends to cut itself off completely from the
Church. For it, as the same observer has remarked, "the
name of Christ now represents nothing more than one
of the myths of a civilization in decline." The personal
virtues which the Church teaches, diligence, thrift, patience, and so on, are repudiated as nothing more than
bourgeois rationalizations of what is useful to the *status
quo*. It is taken for granted, and in most countries not

The Laboring Class

without reason, that in the class struggle the Church will always be on the wrong side.

Today we are faced in the West no less than in the East with what is essentially a missionary situation. So far the churches have shown little sign of realizing the missionary and pioneer nature of their task in the new day. If missionaries are going out to distant lands, they are usually given some technical training. Those who are going to work among Moslems attend lectures on Islam and try to absorb something of the Moslem atmosphere and point of view. Those who are going to simple peoples attend lectures on anthropology and primitive religions. When a missionary arrives in the country where he is to work, he knows that a year's hard work will be needed before he can make his first stumbling efforts at preaching in the language of the people; probably ten times that period will elapse before he feels that he can speak to them with a real understanding of their point of view. If he is breaking new ground, among a people whose language has never been learned by civilized men or reduced to writing, a whole lifetime may be spent in building the first bridges of approach.

The Church has to remind itself today that the great world of the industrial worker is to it almost as much an unknown world as the heart of Central Africa. All those who have tried to explore that world warn us that effective Christian witness can be rendered only from within, and not by approaches which, however sympathetic, are felt to come from without. All who have tried to penetrate that world and to bear Christian witness within it, tell us that the task is extremely difficult.

And yet this is one of the kingdoms of the world that is to be claimed and possessed in the name of Christ.

If the Church is ever to enter in, we shall have to learn to be far more adaptable and experimental in our methods than we are.

One young Canadian minister, who has spent a good deal of time in Germany, told me recently that, if he was going to work permanently in that country, he would take a job in a factory, as the only way of bringing any effective Christian witness into the world of the workers. He feels that the Church is so thoroughly bourgeois that there is no hope at present that the workers can be brought back into it as it is, and, therefore, that the only hope is that the Church should go to the workers where they are, and on the level on which they live. As you may know, in France a number of Roman Catholic priests are now living and working as factory hands with a directly evangelistic purpose.

Others take a rather different view. They feel that there is something unnatural and artificial in the ordained minister working as a factory hand, and that that is not the way really to gain the confidence of the workers. But they recognize that our large buildings, formal services, paid staffs, and all the paraphernalia of a modern parish form a barrier which is almost certain to keep the working man as far away from us as he can get. It may be that we shall have to be willing to return to far simpler conditions, and to abandon a great deal that we have come to value. It may be that we shall have to be willing to work with far smaller groups, more along the lines of the communist cell or the trade union unit—groups small enough for the working man to find himself at home in them, and to feel that he can make his own contribution to their life. "*Query:* how many workers are there on the councils of the elders or the synods?" pertinently asks our French observer.

If you are led to experiment in new methods and new types of evangelism, I cannot hold out to you much hope of encouragement from the leadership in your church. I have every sympathy with the leaders; they have come by experience to trust in well-tried and tested methods; they are concerned with the increasingly difficult task of manning existing churches and maintaining existing work. It is not surprising if they wish to keep you in the strictly conventional paths, and frown on what in the end may prove to be profitless experiments. But the Church has always lived by the courage of those who are prepared to fling their caps over the moon and to attempt what has never been done before. Nine out of ten of them may prove to be poor fools, who had much better never have ventured out at all; the tenth may turn out to be Francis of Assisi or John Wesley. And without such men, the Church will never win its way into this great kingdom, which today is so largely sealed off from its approaches.

VIII

That is the major challenge in the West. But still the greatest of the kingdoms that remain to be won for Christ is that of the non-Christian world.

The situation in relation to foreign missions has radically changed in a hundred years. The miraculous success of the great missionary efforts of the nineteenth century has brought into existence large and flourishing churches in almost every part of the world. The first half of the twentieth century has seen the emancipation of many of these churches from foreign control. The missionary of today goes out not as the leader of the Church to which he is called, but as its servant.

This very success creates the danger that we may lose our sense of proportion as to what still remains to be done. There is a rapid growth of a mythology about the "younger churches" which bears little relation to the facts. The very existence of the "younger churches" is evidence of the miraculous power of God at work today. Yet those churches are small, weak, immature, and still unequal to the many tasks that the situation in their various countries lays upon them. In India, Christians number only 2 per cent of the population. That 2 per cent includes the irregular, the unfaithful, the half-converted, the nominal adherents—all those classes of passengers so familiar in a nominally Christian parish in America. The great majority are simple village and mountain folk. Growth, progress and promise are magnificent. But the task of effectively bearing witness throughout the whole of India is still far beyond the strength of those young churches.

In Japan, much less than 1 per cent of the population is Christian. What has been said of India can be said *a fortiori* of Japan, except that in Japan, in contrast to the village church of India, the greatest strength of Christianity is in the cities.

In the lands of the "younger churches" today there are three areas of urgent need.

The first is in those places where the name of Christ has never yet been named at all. One of the reports presented to the Edinburgh Missionary Conference of 1910 was on "unoccupied fields." If a similar report were to be drawn up today, it would be painfully like that of forty years ago.

Even in a country like India, where missionary work has been carried on for four hundred years, there are still large areas untouched by any presentation of the Gospel. For many years I had felt a special concern for the Indian state of Rewa. This was under an independent ruler, who, as he was entitled to do, had forbidden any Christian evangelistic work in his area. The state was about as large as Holland, with a population of some two million. It was in every way backward, only 2 per cent of the people being literate. Through the chance that a cousin of mine was appointed by the government of India as chief minister of the state, I once spent a weekend in Rewa city, and held the first Christian service which had taken place there in many years. The total congregation was five including myself. Now the ban on evangelistic work has at last been withdrawn. A small group of Indian Lutheran missionaries has moved over the border from the southeast, and begun the work of proclaiming the Gospel in that hitherto unreached area. You will remember that the population which that small group of workers is trying to reach is about the same as the population of Connecticut, a fact worth bearing in mind, when people press upon you the urgent need for man power in the American churches.

Secondly, there is the urgency of the situation, where the growth of the churches is far too rapid to be directed or controlled by the forces available at the present time. During my recent tour in Africa, one of the Anglican bishops said to me, "If I could stop the Christian movement in this area, I would." New converts were crowding in at the rate of 8,000 a year. He already had under his care something like 200,000 Christians, living in 1,473 centers. His total staff of ordained ministers was just fifty, Africans and Europeans included, and a number of these were engaged in teaching or administrative work. In such a situation, there are only three possibilities. One is, as the bishop suggested, to refuse to accept any more converts. The result of this would probably be the setting up of hurriedly devised native churches, on a mixed basis of half-understood Christianity and traditional paganism. The second is to take in those who apply, and to give them the best training possible with the available resources, knowing well that such inadequate training is likely to produce in two generations a static and self-complacent Christianity, which is sometimes harder to move than paganism itself. The third possibility, of course, would be to double the number of missionaries immediately, and of African ministers within ten years; but that would seem to presuppose the miracle of the "older churches" waking up for the first time to take their missionary responsibilities really seriously.

The third field of urgency is in the training of the ministry for the "younger churches." All the churches and missions are now pledged to a policy of "devolution," that is, the transference of control in the "younger churches" from the home boards and organizations in distant countries to the leaders of the Church in the field. This process is going forward with what in some areas might be called dangerous rapidity, and heavy burdens of responsibility are being laid upon those who have had only the most sketchy training for them. If it is possible during this time of transition to develop in the "younger churches" a competent and spiritually effective ministry, then those churches will stand and grow; if not, they may well be heading for disaster. The situation is developing apace and will not wait; what is done in twenty years from now may come much too late to meet the need.

We are constantly told today that there is no essential difference between the home front and what we used to call the mission field. In general I agree. But, if it is still permitted to make a comparison, I would say that in point of urgency, every post in the mission field has far stronger claims than the corresponding post at home.

I have limited my examples to the theological sphere, because you happen to be theological students. Just the same would apply in many other spheres. I have recently visited a great many theological schools in Africa. In one of them I found that the entire staff consisted of one missionary, and one African, the African having had no training at all, except a course in the seminary in which he is now a teacher. That school has a library of less than a thousand volumes. Even if it had more, they would be of value to the staff only, since most of the students have not enough knowledge of English to enable them to read an ordinary theological book, and the staff has in consequence to face the immense labor of getting everything across to them in their African language. Compare that with the conditions obtaining in the least well staffed and equipped of the seminaries from which you come, and the contrast is horrifying.

It may be said that when students are on the intellectual level of most African candidates for the ministry there is no need of a large staff and elaborate equipment for them. This is only partly true. On the whole, the work which the African ordained minister will have to do will be more difficult than that which will be committed to you, if you stay in America. You will have one or two churches; he will have anything up to fifty. Your people will be to some extent homogeneous in education and point of view; his may include everything from the graduate of a Western university, with all kinds of intellectual doubts and questionings about the Christian faith, down to the simple illiterate peasant woman, just emerging out of the darkness of untouched paganism. Your people have the background of an at least partially Christian culture; your African brother will be dealing the whole time with the clash in the minds of his people and of his churches between Christian teaching and pagan presuppositions. You will be able to refresh yourself constantly through contact with other ministers and through books, papers and magazines; the African will live in conditions of extreme isolation, with all the cooling influences of paganism and superstition round him; he may have little to rely on for intellectual stimulus beyond the notes which he himself took in his seminary days.

Which of you needs the better and more careful training? On which of you ought the churches to be pouring out more of their resources and their brains? Make your own comparisons and form your own judgments. There is no doubt at all in my own mind as to the answer I would give.

IX

Obviously it is not possible for everyone to seek a vocation in the work of the Church overseas. Not everyone is qualified; not everyone is physically fit; not everyone is called. The question is simply one of wholehearted obedience to the will of God, as he is pleased to

Foreign missionary field

reveal it. He cannot reveal to us the fullness of his will, if we by previous choices of our own, or simple acquiescence in a course of action that circumstances seem to have laid down for us, eliminate in advance three-quarters of the possibilities that he might have in mind for us.

It is this that makes it so important that both we as individuals, and the Church itself, should constantly ascend the mount of vision, which is also the mount of temptation, and survey the whole world scene as it is spread out before us in the changing panorama of history. Temptations may be of various sorts. When the Church is strong, the temptation may be to confident arrogance, and even to the use of the powers of the world to subdue the world to Christ. When the Church is well established, the temptation may be to a complacency which rests on such a security and expectancy of progress as God has never in fact promised to his Church. When the Church is weak, the temptation may be to fear and dismay, in the face of the gathering forces of darkness. Victory comes with the recognition of the nature of the task that God has given us. Christ's lordship is already a fact. That lordship will finally be manifested when God has fulfilled the purpose which he is working out in the history of men. In the long interim, our task is to share in the obedience of the Christ, to proclaim his lordship with power, to resist all that denies it, to win men and women into the fellowship which manifests it, to stand firm to the end, and not to be afraid.

For the mount of temptation can also become the mount of Transfiguration. The Transfiguration was concerned both with the decease which Christ was to accomplish at Jerusalem, and with the glory which should be revealed thereafter. It sets forth the close connection between obedience and glory. We, as followers of Christ, are called to like obedience. We are also called, as we have seen, to gaze on Christ, until we too are transfigured from glory to glory, even as by the Lord of the Spirit. We read in the Gospels that a cloud covered the mount of the Transfiguration, and that the disciples feared as they entered into the cloud. But when they had entered into it, they found that Jesus was with them also in the cloud.